FINANCIAL SECTOR OF THE AMERICAN ECONOMY

edited by

STUART BRUCHEY
UNIVERSITY OF MAINE

A GARLAND SERIES

THE EFFECTS OF REAL EXCHANGE RATE VOLATILITY ON SECTORAL INVESTMENT

EMPIRICAL EVIDENCE FROM FIXED AND FLEXIBLE EXCHANGE RATE SYSTEMS

BAHAR ERDAL

GARLAND PUBLISHING, INC.
NEW YORK & LONDON / 1997

Library of Congress Cataloging-in-Publication Data

Erdal, Bahar, 1964–
    The effects of real exchange rate volatility on sectoral invest-
ment : empirical evidence from fixed and flexible exchange rate
systems / Bahar Erdal.
        p.   cm. — (Financial sector of the American economy)
    Includes bibliographical references and index.
    ISBN 0-8153-2922-9 (alk. paper)
    1. Foreign exchange administration—European Union
countries. 2. Investments—European Union countries. 3. Foreign
exchange rates—European Union countries. I. Title. II. Series.
HG3942.E73 1997
332.6—dc21   97-23135

Printed on acid-free, 250-year-life paper
Manufactured in the United States of America

To my parents, Hüseyin and Gönül Erdal

Contents

Chapter

List of Tables

Preface

What are the effects of real exchange rate volatility on sectoral investment in the fixed and flexible exchange rate systems. This is originally the topic of my Ph.D. dissertation under the supervision of Professor Stacie Beck at the University of Delaware.

After the collapse of Bretton Woods fixed exchange rate system, negative implications of real exchange rate volatility led European countries to adopt a quasi-fixed exchange rate system, which is called the Exchange Rate Mechanism of the European Monetary System. The main reason for adoption of the quasi-fixed exchange rate system was to create a stable exchange rate environment, and by that to induce investment and trade in Europe. Since I have found no empirical study about the effects of real exchange rate volatility on sectoral investment in Europe, it is impossible to make any decision about the success of the European Monetary System in this field.

The objective of this study is to test empirically the effects of the levels and volatility of real exchange rates on investment in the manufacturing sectors of the countries in the European Monetary System, as well as of the countries in the flexible exchange rate system. Volatility can be transferred from exchange rates to interest rates. Real interest rate volatility is another source of uncertainty and also depressing effects on investment spending. Therefore, another contribution of this study is this additional empirical evidence about the effects of real interest rate volatility on sectoral investment in Europe.

In the empirical part of the study, the hypothesis is tested using annual time-series data pooled across sectors for each country separately. Annual data at the sectoral level were obtained for Belgium, Denmark, Finland, France, Germany, Italy, the Netherlands, Norway, the United Kingdom, and the United States from the OECD. The estimation period covers the period 1973 to 1993.

The empirical results provide that real exchange rate volatility has depressing effects on sectoral investment in the flexible exchange rate system, and has no depressing effects on sectoral investment in the European Monetary System. The empirical results do not show any conclusive evidence concerning volatility transfer from exchange rates to interest rates.

While the existing studies do not show any depressing effects of real exchange rate volatility on investment spending, the empirical results of this study show negatively significant effects of real exchange rate volatility on investment spending.

Acknowledgments

I would like to thank a number of people who helped me complete this research. Their assistance has come in various forms: refinement of ideas and criticism; inspiration and moral support; and help with research and financial support.

First, I would like to express my gratitude to the Department of Economics at the University of Delaware for the opportunity to further my studies in economics. I would especially like to thank my advisor Dr. Stacie Beck for her continued advisement, encouragement, support, and quidance during the two years. Her meticulous reviews followed by excellent suggestions have helped me to understand the complexity of my work.

I would like to thank members of my dissertation committee: Dr. Sridhar Iyer, Dr. Toni M. Whited, and Dr. Janet Todd for their active participation and useful feedback in the research. I especially want to thank Dr. Toni M. Whited for her guidance about investment theory, and Dr. Sridhar Iyer for encouraging me to pursue a Ph.D. in economics. I would also like to thank Dr. Pamela Smith for her insightful suggestions throughout my research.

I would like to extend my thanks Dr. Linda S. Goldberg of New York University, and Janice C. Eberly of the Wharton Business School for their excellent suggestions which helped me to improve my research.

I would like to thank Dr. Ernur Demir Abaan and Neşe Özer for their helpful suggestions. I want to express my gratitude to Dr. Ahmet N. Kıpıcı for his valuable comments and helps throughout preparation of the manuscript.

I would also like to thank Dr. Stuart Bruchey, professor of history at the University of Maine, for seeing value in this research and making a commitment to realize this book.

I am grateful to Anita Kandhalam, Nicole Richardson, Sibel Gök, and Rajaram Ghana for their friendship and constant encouragement. At this time, I can express my sincere thanks to my brother, Ertuğrul Erdal, for his support.

My parents have played a very important role in my academic pursuits. Their love, understanding, and unwavering support made it possible for me to take this academic challenge. I could not achieve this goal without them.

Dr. Bahar Erdal

The Effects of Real Exchange Rate Volatility on Sectoral Investment

I

Introduction

The Exchange Rate Mechanism (ERM) of the European Monetary System (EMS)[1] adopted a target zone system in March 1979, because the flexible exchange rates were too volatile. The ERM provides that each participating currency has a central rate expressed in terms of the European Currency Unit (ECU), an index based on member currencies, and the currencies cannot deviate from their central rates beyond a margin of +/- 2.25 percent. When the currency deviates from its central rate beyond the margins, its ECU rate is redefined by realignments, and revaluation (or devaluation) of the currencies are determined in order to eliminate changes in relative price levels.

Although the ERM experience introduces a new kind of volatility, volatility caused by the expectations of the realignments, Engel and Hakkio (1993) showed that the real exchange rate volatility in the ERM is smaller when compared with that in the flexible exchange rate system.

One of the main reasons for the establishment of the ERM of the EMS was to create a stable exchange rate environment, and by that to induce investment and trade in Europe. Artis and Taylor (1994), and Grauwe and Verfaille (1988) showed that the EMS was successful in reducing real exchange rate volatility. Grauwe and Verfaille (1988) also showed that the EMS helped to increase trade between the EMS versus non-EMS countries instead of intra-EMS trade. Since no empirical study has been done about the effects of real exchange rate volatility on the European investment, it is not possible to talk about the effects of real exchange rate volatility on investment in Europe.

This study analyzes the effects of real exchange rate volatility on investment in manufacturing sectors for countries under quasi-fixed (that is, the EMS) and flexible exchange rate systems, by answering the question, "In which system does real exchange rate volatility have depressing effects on sectoral investment?"

This study can help to determine whether adopting an exchange rate system like the ERM of the EMS is worthwhile for non-EMS countries.

Since, exchange rates fluctuate within narrow margins in the quasi-fixed exchange rate system, real exchange rate volatility should not have depressing effects on sectoral investment. On the other hand, in the flexible exchange rate system, exchange rates fluctuate randomly, so, real exchange rate volatility should have depressing effects on sectoral investment.

Theoretically, real exchange rate volatility can have important effects on domestic and foreign investment decisions. Real exchange rate volatility changes the international competitiveness of the countries, causes reallocation of resources among the sectors, causes relocation of resources across countries, and creates an uncertain environment for investment decisions if the investments are irreversible. Krugman (1989) states that

> Uncertainty creates an incentive for firms to pursue a "wait and see" attitude, widening the range of no change in which firms neither enter nor exit. And now we come to the important point: The incentive not to act is greater the more volatile the exchange rate. It is a straightforward result from option pricing that the ratio of the market price at which an option is exercised to the strike price is higher the greater is market volatility. Similarly, in the sunk cost model a firm will wait for a more favorable exchange rate before entering, and will remain in the market for a more unfavorable rate, the greater the perceived future uncertainty of the rate.[2]

A theoretical study by Aizenman (1992) showed that both domestic and foreign investments are higher in a fixed exchange rate system. There are few empirical studies about the effects of both real exchange rates and real exchange rate volatility on investment. Just as empirical studies give ambiguous results about the relation between the changes in real exchange rates and investment expenditures, they also do not show clear correspondence of the effects of real exchange rate volatility on investment expenditures.

Empirical evidence by Goldberg (1993) showed that the U.S. dollar appreciations (depreciations) during the 1980s caused investment expansions (contractions) in the U.S. durable goods manufacturing and nonmanufacturing sectors, and mixed effects in nondurable goods manufacturing sectors. Luehrman (1991) found that depreciation of domestic currency did not increase international competitiveness of the firms in the auto and steel industries of the G-7 countries. Froot and Stein (1991) showed that real exchange rate movements are not strong enough to affect foreign direct investment inflows into the United States as well as into the United Kingdom, Germany, Canada, and Japan.

On the other hand, Campa and Goldberg (1995) and Goldberg (1993) showed that real exchange rate volatility had no substantial depressing effects on the investment in U.S. industry. Goldberg (1993) also indicated that real exchange rate volatility led to investment expansions in durable goods manufacturing sectors in the 1970s and investment contractions in the 1980s.

Pindyck and Solimano (1993) concluded that the inflation rate has negative and statistically significant effects on aggregate investment expenditures, while real exchange rate volatility does not have depressing effects for data pooled across countries. Pindyck and Solimano (1993) used pooled aggregate investment data, which may mask different patterns at the sectoral level. For instance, exporting industries are likely to react differently than the importing industries to changes in real exchange rates.

Campa and Goldberg (1995) and Goldberg (1993) addressed this issue by using sectoral investment data. Goldberg's studies used only U.S. data. Since the U.S. is large and has a relatively closed economy, the response of investment decisions to exchange rate levels or volatility may not be very high.

The objective of this study is to test the effects of the levels and volatility of real exchange rates on investment in manufacturing sectors for open economies. Pindyck and Solimano (1993) state that

> Future work in improving this data and extending it to the sectoral level is needed. . .nor have we examined possible differences in the effects of instability on different types of investment (e.g., equipment versus structures).[3]

Annual data at the sectoral level was obtained for Belgium, Denmark, Finland, France, Germany, Italy, the Netherlands, Norway, the United Kingdom, and the United States for the period 1979 to 1993 from the Organization for Economic Cooperation and Development (OECD). To the best of my knowledge, this data has not been used in a study of real investment behavior elsewhere.

A comparison of the impact the exchange rate system has on the relationship between real exchange rates and sectoral investment can be made since Belgium, Denmark, France, Germany, Italy, and the Netherlands are in the quasi-fixed exchange rate system (that is, the EMS) and Finland, Norway, the United Kingdom, and the United States are in the flexible exchange rate system.[4] The United States is also included for comparison to previous studies.

For four countries: Finland, Germany, the United Kingdom, and the United States foreign trade data as well as investment data are available at the sectoral level. Sector-specific foreign trade data provide the opportunity to analyze the effect export and import exposure of the sector has in its sensitivity to real exchange rate levels and volatility. A second stage of estimation is carried out for these countries that includes variables measuring the "openness" of each sector.

Exchange rate management has implications for the behavior of interest rates. A reduction in real exchange rate volatility may cause real interest rate volatility to rise. In other words, volatility can be transferred from exchange rates to interest rates. Theoretically, interest rate volatility creates another source of uncertainty, which has an adverse effect on the level of real investment (Ingersoll and Ross, 1992). I have not found an empirical study about the effects of real interest rate volatility on European investment.

Therefore, another contribution of this study is this additional empirical evidence on the effects of real interest rate volatility and inflation rate volatility on sectoral investment in Europe.

The procedure of this study is as follows:

In Chapter 2, investment theories under certainty and uncertainty are explained, and theoretical and empirical studies about investment under uncertainty are presented. Then the effects of both changes in levels and volatility of the real exchange rates on real investment are explained theoretically, and empirical studies are presented.

In Chapter 3, the value of the plant and the value of the option to invest in the plant under real exchange rate uncertainty are determined for export-oriented and import-competing firms, as well as import-oriented firms using option pricing techniques. Investment equations and variable descriptions, which are used in the empirical part of the study in Chapters 5 and 6, are then presented.

Chapter 4 presents a detailed description of data sources and definitions, followed by the construction of cross-sectional time-series data. Then, construction of the dependent and independent variables used in Chapters 5 and 6 is explained.

In Chapter 5, the estimation results excluding export and import exposure of the sectors are reported for the EMS countries and countries in the flexible exchange rate system.

Chapter 6 reports the estimation results including export and import exposure of the sectors.

Chapter 7 summarizes the estimation results and presents conclusions.

NOTES

1. The European Monetary System became the European Economic and Monetary Union (EMU) by the Maastricht Treaty in February 1992.

2. Paul Krugman, *Exchange Rate Instability* (Cambridge, MA: The MIT Press, 1989), p. 54

3. Robert S. Pindyck and Andres Solimano, "Economic Instability and Aggregate Investment," *NBER Macroeconomics Annual* (Cambridge, MA: The MIT Press, 1993), p. 298.

4. The United Kingdom was also a member of the EMS. However, the United Kingdom did not join the ERM of the EMS until October 1990, therefore, it is considered in the flexible exchange rate system.

II

Survey of the Literature

2.1 Introduction

Business investment is a key determinant of economic growth. But, why some countries invest more than the others, or what are the factors that affect investment decisions of the firms are the questions those should be answered by the economists and econometricians.

In the investment literature, there are several theories that explain the investment decisions of firms. These theories can be divided into two groups: investment theories under certainty and investment theories under uncertainty. While past theories built investment theories under certainty, recent literature gives more attention to investment under uncertainty.

The procedure of this chapter is as follows:

In Section 2.2, the investment theories under certainty are explained.

In Section 2.3, the investment theories under uncertainty are explained, then both theoretical and empirical studies about the investment under uncertainty are presented.

In Section 2.4, the effects of the real exchange rates and real exchange rate volatility on investment decisions are described, and empirical studies about the effects of real exchange rates and real exchange rate volatility on investment decisions of firms are presented.

In Section 2.5, summary and implications drawn from the literature survey are reported.

2.2   Investment Under Certainty

There are four conventional investment theories under certainty: the Marginal Efficiency of Capital, the Accelerator theory, the Neoclassical theory, and the Tobin's marginal q theory. In this section these theories are described briefly.

The first attempt to explain the investment behavior of firms was made by John Maynard Keynes during the 1930s. Keynes (1936) states that optimal investment is attained when marginal efficiency of capital is equal to the market interest rate. Marginal efficiency of capital depends on the prospective returns of capital, not the current return of capital. Keynes (1936) describes the determination of marginal efficiency of capital as follows:

> When a man buys an investment or capital asset, he purchases the right to the series of prospective returns, which he expects to obtain from selling its output, after deducting the running expenses of obtaining that output during the life of the asset. This series of annuities Q1, Q2,. . .Qn it is convenient to call the prospective yield of the investment. Over against the prospective yield of investment we have the supply price of the capital asset, meaning by this, not the market price at which an asset of the type question can actually be purchased in the market, but the price which would just induce a manufacturer newly to produce an additional unit of such assets, i.e., what is sometimes called replacement cost. The relation between prospective yield of a capital asset and its supply price or replacement cost, i.e., the relation between the prospective of one more unit of that type of capital and the cost of producing that unit, furnishes us with the marginal efficiency of capital of that type. More precisely, I define the marginal efficiency of capital as being equal to that rate of discount which would make the present value of the series of annuities given by the returns expected from the

capital asset during its life just equal to its supply price. This gives us the marginal efficiencies of particular types of capital assets.[1]

Therefore, if the marginal efficiency of capital is greater than the market interest rate, the investment will increase until the optimal rate of investment is reached.

The post-Keynesian investment literature begins with the *acceleration principle*. As Serven and Solimano (1992) noted, this theory became prevalent in the 1950s and early 1960s. Today, it is still used today for growth models and in investment models.[2]

According to the accelerator-principle theory, investment is a linear function of the changes in output. This theory rests on some strict assumptions. Duesenberry (1958) explains these assumptions as follows:

- There is an optimal production method for each product that is not affected by the interest rates.

- Products are produced at fixed proportions with respect to changes in income levels.

- At fixed interest rates (or approximately fixed), each firm can increase its capital stock as much as it wants.

- The optimal production method requires a certain amount of capital.

- Relative prices are fixed with respect to income changes.

- At time *t*, each firm invests until it equalizes its capital stock to the optimal capital for the income at *t - 1*.

Let I_t be the net investment at time t, Y_{t-1} the income at time $t - 1$, and K_{t-1} capital stock at the end of time $t - 1$. Then net investment is

$$I_t = \beta Y_{t-1} - K_{t-1} \tag{2.1}$$

where β is the coefficient that measures the optimal amount of capital per unit of output. According to last assumption, capital stock at the end of time $t - 1$ is optimal for output at time $t - 2$. Therefore,

$$K_{t-1} = \beta Y_{t-2} \tag{2.2}$$

substituting equation (2.2) into equation (2.1) gives

$$I_t = \beta Y_{t-1} - \beta Y_{t-2} = \beta (Y_{t-1} - Y_{t-2}) \tag{2.3}$$

Equation (2.3) shows that the net investment at time t is a function of the difference of the income at time $t - 1$ and income at $t - 2$.

As can be seen from equation (2.3), the acceleration principle does not include the effects of exogenous changes in net investment (that is, changes in investment due to technological developments). If exogenous changes are in the form of autonomous investment (I_a), the net investment equation is represented as

$$I_t = \beta (Y_{t-1} - Y_{t-2}) + I_a \tag{2.4}$$

Since, gross investment is the sum of net investment and autonomous investment, equation (2.4) can be treated as the gross investment (I_g) equation

$$I_g = \beta (Y_{t-1} - Y_{t-2}) + I_a \tag{2.5}$$

Equation (2.5) indicates that gross investment is a function of changes in output.

The Neoclassical theory was developed by Dale W. Jorgenson during the 1960s. The studies of Jorgenson (1963, 1967) and Hall and Jorgenson (1971) provide significant contributions to this theory.

The Neoclassical theory is based on the theory of optimal capital accumulation, which is determined by the maximization of the present value of net cash flows. This theory is also called the Neoclassical Theory of Optimal Capital Accumulation.

This theory makes the optimal level of investment a function of the output prices, output, and user cost of capital (which is also called the implicit rental value of capital). The user cost of capital is determined by the real interest rate, the prices of investment goods, and the depreciation rate.

The user cost of capital is explained intuitively as follows: assume an investment good is purchased. By buying the investment good, the firm loses interest, that is, if the firm were put its capital in a bank, the capital would earn interest that is equal to the cost of investment good multiplied by the interest rate. In addition, the investment good depreciates each year by an amount proportional to depreciation rate. On the other hand, capital gains occur from the increases in the value of the investment good. So, the user cost of capital is equal to the sum of the interest loss and the depreciation loss, less the capital gains. When the inflation rate acts as a proxy for the capital gain, the user cost of capital is a function of the real interest rate, the price of the investment good, and the depreciation rate.

The Neoclassical theory is explained in two stages. At the first stage, the optimal level of capital stock is determined at the equilibrium where the marginal revenue product of capital is equal to the user cost of capital (that is, marginal cost of capital). At the second stage, the investment demand function is derived, depending on the optimal level of capital stock. Since the realization of investment decisions take time, investment demand is equal to the difference between desired capital stock in period *t* and period *t - 1*, plus actual capital stock.[3]

According to the *Tobin's marginal q theory*, investment spending is positively related to the ratio of the market value of an additional unit of capital to its replacement cost. Investment increases when marginal q exceeds unity, and decreases when marginal q is less than unity. Since measuring marginal q empirically is difficult, empirical studies use average q as a proxy. Average q is the ratio of the market value of the firm to the replacement cost of its assets.

Hayashi (1982) proves that marginal q equals average q, under the assumptions that the firm is a price taker and that the production function and the installation function are homogenous.

2.3   Investment Under Uncertainty

While the old theories assume investment decisions are made with certainty, recent investment literature introduces uncertainty into the investment models. As explained by Pindyck (1991), previous theories ignore two important characteristics of investment expenditures.

First, most investment expenditures are irreversible, which means they are sunk costs, and cannot be recovered.

Second, investments can be delayed creating the option of waiting for new information about prices, costs, and other market conditions.

Irreversibility and the option of waiting for new information make investors sensitive to uncertainties about macroeconomic variables. Pindyck (1991) states that

> Investment spending on an aggregate level may be highly sensitive to risk in various forms: uncertainties over future product prices and input costs that directly determine cash flows, uncertainty over exchange rates, and uncertainty over future tax and regulatory policy. This means that if a goal of macroeconomic policy is to stimulate investment, stability and credibility may be more important than the particular levels of tax rates or interest rates. Put another way, if uncertainty over the economic environment is high, tax and related incentives may have to be very large to have any significant impact on investment.[4]

Irreversibility of real investment also explains *hysteresis* in trade, which is defined as "the tendency for an effect (such as foreign sales in the United States) to persist well after the cause that brought it about (an appreciation of the dollar) has disappeared."[5] For instance, the U.S. dollar appreciations during the 1980s caused foreign firms to enter the U.S. markets. However, entering a market requires sunk costs such as marketing, advertisement, research and development expenditures, etc. Therefore, despite the subsequent depreciation of the U.S. dollar, foreign firms stayed in the U.S. market by absorbing their losses because of their sunk costs.[6]

2.3.1 *Theoretical Studies About Investment Under Uncertainty*

The literature on investment under uncertainty consists mostly of theoretical studies. These studies derive different conclusions about the sign of the investment-uncertainty relationship. While Abel (1983) and Caballero (1991) find a positive relationship, Craine (1989) finds a negative relationship between investment and uncertainty. Ingersoll and Ross (1992) using option pricing techniques show that real interest rate uncertainty has depressing effects on investment decisions of firms.

Abel (1983) investigates the effect of output price uncertainty on the risk-neutral firm's investment decisions. It is assumed that the competitive firm has a symmetric, convex cost of adjustments and Cobb-Douglas production function. The optimal rate of investment is the rate at which the marginal cost of investment is equal to the marginal valuation of capital. The optimal rate of investment is an increasing function of the slope of the value function, which is equal to the present value of expected marginal revenue product of capital. For a competitive firm with constant returns to scale production function, the slope of the value function depends on the price of output and variance of the price of output. So, the optimal rate of investment is independent of capital.

The effect of uncertainty on investment can be determined by analyzing the effect of uncertainty on the slope of the value function. Under perfect competition, the marginal revenue product of capital is a strictly convex function of the price of output. Assume that the price of output is given. If the uncertainty is measured by the variance of the price of output, then an increase in uncertainty about future prices of output will increase the expected future marginal revenue product of capital and by that the optimal rate of investment. It is concluded that if the marginal revenue product of capital is a convex function of the price of output, the expected value of this marginal revenue product of capital is an increasing function of the variance of the price of output (that is, uncertainty).

Caballero (1991) extends Abel (1983) by introducing asymmetric costs (asymmetric means that increasing capital can be cheaper than decreasing it) of adjustment to allow for irreversibility and decreasing marginal return to capital. Decreasing marginal return to capital can be caused by either imperfect competition or decreasing returns to scale, or both. Under the assumptions of perfect competition, risk-neutrality, and constant returns to scale, it is proven that there is a positive relationship between uncertainty and investment with asymmetric adjustment costs. Therefore, it is concluded that, the convexity of the marginal profitability of capital with respect to prices of output is the main factor effecting the sign of investment-uncertainty relationship. On the other hand, imperfect competition (or decreasing returns to scale) can cause a negative investment-uncertainty relation.

It should also be noted that both Abel (1983) and Caballero (1991) assume constant returns to scale and perfect competition. These assumptions make the marginal revenue product of capital independent of capital stock. For that reason, the firm cannot consider its future capital stock, therefore irreversibility, when deciding how much to invest today.

Craine (1989) tries to solve the conflict between the economic and finance literature, regarding the sign of the investment-uncertainty relationship. According to the economic literature, higher price uncertainty causes higher costs of investment projects. Therefore, investment increases at the present period (that is, Abel, 1983). In the finance literature, however, an increase in the risk of the asset decreases the demand for this asset. Assuming firms are risk-averse, it is proven that a negative relationship exists between uncertainty and investment. That is, uncertainty decreases investment.

Finally, *Ingersoll and Ross (1992)* examine the impacts of the real interest rate level and real interest rate uncertainty on irreversible investment decisions of the firms. It is assumed that, real interest rates are stochastic and future cash flows are deterministic. It is shown that under real interest rate uncertainty, every project has an option value of waiting whether it has deterministic cash flows or not.

According to finance theory, the firm should invest at the break-even interest rate (that is, internal rate of return), which equates the net present value of the project to zero. Under uncertainty, however, the firm should invest when the real interest rate is equal to an acceptance interest rate, which is less than the break-even interest rate. An increase in uncertainty decreases the acceptance interest rate, so the difference between the break-even interest rate and the acceptance interest rate widens.

Since, in such an environment, the firm is willing to wait for new information about real interest rates, investment is not realized. They also show that, long-term projects have higher volatility, and therefore, higher option value of waiting compared to short-term projects.

Additionally, Ingersoll and Ross's study proves that a reduction in real interest rates may not always increase investment. A reduction in the real interest rates may also decrease the cost of waiting to invest. Consequently, if the firm wants to wait for lower interest rates, investment does not occur.

2.3.2   Empirical Studies About the Investment Under Uncertainty

Empirical studies about the investment uncertainty relationship are few. Pindyck (1991) explains this issue as follows:

> The existing literature on these effects of uncertainty and instability is a largely theoretical one. This may reflect the fact that models of irreversible investment under uncertainty are relatively complicated, and so are difficult to translate into well-specified empirical models. In any case, the gap here between theory and empiricism is disturbing. While it is clear from the theory that increases in the volatility of, say, interest rates or exchange rates should depress investment, it is not at all clear how large these effects should be. Nor is it clear how important these factors have been as explanators of investment across countries and over time. Most econometric models of aggregate economic activity ignore the role of risk, or deal with it only implicitly. A more explicit treatment of risk may help to better explain economic fluctuations, and especially investment spending. [7]

Recent empirical studies are summarized below :

Leahy and Whited (1996) provide empirical findings on the investment-uncertainty relationship. Uncertainty is measured by the variance of the firm's stock return for each year. The data is the U.S. firm-level panel data from COMPUSTAT manufacturing files. The estimation period covers the period 1981 to 1987 for 772 manufacturing firms.

The estimation results show that uncertainty decreases the investment if the investment is irreversible. Leahy and Whited do not find any evidence that uncertainty increases investment by the convexity of the marginal product of capital or by the presence of a capital asset pricing model (CAPM)-based effect of risk.

Ferderer (1993) explores the effects of uncertainty on aggregate investment spending in the United States from the period 1969:3 through 1989:1. Then he compares the explanatory power of uncertainty on investment spending with that of the Neoclassical, and Tobin's average q investment models.

In this study, uncertainty is measured by the risk premium in the term structure of interest rates. Assuming market risk price is positive, the risk premium reflects uncertainty about future interest rates and other macroeconomic variables. The bond buyer rate and treasury bill rate risk premia are used in the estimations.

First, the relationship between the risk premia and four interest rate uncertainty proxies are examined by regressing the risk premia on uncertainty proxies and quality spread. Uncertainty proxies are the six-month moving variances of the Bond Buyer and three-month Treasury bill rate changes; and four-quarter moving averages of the absolute Goldsmith-Nagan forecast errors for the Bond Buyer and three-month Treasury bill rates. While the first two proxies measure the volatility of actual interest rates, the last two measure the size of the recent forecast errors. The quality spread is the spread between AAA and BAA corporate bond rates. The estimation results show that there is a positive relationship between the risk premia and uncertainty proxies. The risk premium reflects uncertainty about interest rates and other macroeconomic variables.

Second, the effect of uncertainty on aggregate investment spending are examined by including lagged values of the risk premia into the Neoclassical and average q models. Aggregate investment spending is measured by the real gross expenditures on producers' durable equipment and the real value of contracts and orders for new plant and equipment. The results indicates that risk premia have negative and statistically significant effects on both types of investment spending.

The estimation results also provides that uncertainty, measured by the risk premium, has more explanatory power on investment spending than the Neoclassical and the average q investment models.

Pindyck and Solimano (1993) test the investment-uncertainty relationship for thirty countries that include 14 less developed countries (LDCs) and 16 Organization for Economic Cooperation and Development (OECD) countries for the full sample period (1962 to 1989) and three sub-periods (1962 to1971, 1972 to 1980, 1981 to 1989).

This paper empirically tests the theory of irreversible investment under uncertainty developed by McDonald and Siegel (1986), Pindyck (1991), Dixit (1992), Pindyck and Dixit (1994), and Caballero and Pindyck (1995). The theory of irreversible investment under uncertainty assumes that investments are irreversible and can be delayed to wait for new information about prices, cost, and other macroeconomic variables.

In these papers, it is shown that irreversible investment is like a financial call option. When the opportunity to undertake irreversible investment is "exercised," it kills the option of investing and the possibility of waiting for new information. This lost option is an opportunity cost for the firm and must be added to the present value of the expected future cash flows in the net present value (NPV) rule. The firm should invest when the expected value of future cash flows exceeds the cost of capital by the amount of this opportunity cost.

Pindyck and Solimano (1993) show that if investment is irreversible and exogenous stochastic variables follow a Brownian motion process,[8] uncertainty can be measured by the volatility of the marginal productivity of capital (MRPK). The volatility of the MRPK also follows a Brownian motion process. An increase in uncertainty increases the required rate of return for investment (that is, threshold) and investment spending decreases.

Pindyck and Solimano's (1993) study presents a very detailed analysis of the effects of uncertainty on investment spending. The relationship between the uncertainty, measured by the volatility of the MRPK, and threshold proxies are examined over the entire sample period. Four proxies for the threshold are calculated from the maximum values of the MRPK, then the relationship between these threshold proxies and the volatility and average growth rates of the MRPK (that is, the drift rate) are examined. Volatility of the MRPK is equal to the standard deviation of the annual log arithmetic change in the MRPK, and the average growth rate of the MRPK is equal to the mean of the annual log arithmetic change in the MRPK. It is expected that volatility is positively related to the threshold and average growth rates are negatively related to the threshold.

The relationship between the rate of private investment (that is, the ratio of private investment to the real gross domestic product (GDP)) and volatility of the MRPK is examined for the LDCs and OECD countries separately. A negative relationship between the rate of private investment and volatility of the MRPK is expected.

Thirdly, the effects of both volatility and average growth rate of the MRPK on real interest rates are examined by running panel regressions. It is expected that an increase in volatility or decrease in the average growth rate of the MRPK should lower the real interest rates, because the investment curve has shifted to the left.

Then the sources of the volatility of the MRPK are investigated. Cross-sectional correlation of standard deviation of MRPK with economic and political instability indicators are estimated for both the LDCs and OECD countries. Economic instability indicators are the mean inflation rate, the average annual standard deviation of the change in the inflation rate, the average annual standard deviation of the change in the real exchange rate, and the average annual standard deviation of the change in interest rates. Political instability indicators are the annual probability of a change in government, the average number of political assassinations, government crises, strikes, riots, revolutions, and constitutional changes per year. Explanatory powers of the economic and political instability indicators over the volatility of MRPK are examined by running a regression for the volatility of the MRPK over the economic and political instability indicators.

Finally, the relationship between aggregate investment and economic instability indicators are examined for six low- (that is, France, Germany, Japan, The Netherlands, the United Kingdom, and the United States), and six high-inflation (that is, Argentina, Bolivia, Brazil, Chile, Israel, and Mexico) countries using annual cross-sectional time-series data from the period 1960 to 1990. Investment data is taken from the national records. The regression equation is as follows:

$$(I \,/\, GDP)_{i,t} = a_1 \, INF_{i,t} + a_2 \, SDINF_{i,t} + a_3 \, SDER_{i,t} + a_4 \, GRTH_{i,t-1}$$
$$+ \, a_5 \, (I \,/\, GDP)_{i,t-1} + e_{i,t}$$

where

$(I\,/\,GDP)_{i,t}$	= ratio of investment to GDP in country i in year t
$INF_{i,t}$	= mean inflation rate for the year t
$SDINF_{i,t}$	= sample standard deviation of each year's monthly observations of inflation
$SDER_{i,t}$	= sample standard deviation of each year's monthly observations of real exchange rate
$GRTH_{i,,t-1}$	= lag of the growth rate of the real GDP
$(I\,/\,GDP)_{i,t-1}$	= lag of the dependent variable
$e_{i,t}$	= disturbance term

Estimation results support the theory that uncertainty, that is proxied by the volatility of the MRPK, increases threshold proxies. Drift rates, that is proxied by the average growth rate of the MRPK, decrease threshold proxies. The estimation results also show that the volatility of the MRPK has negative significant effects on the rate of investment of the LDCs and has no effects on the rate of investment of the OECD countries. The volatility of the MRPK affects the real interest rates negatively. This negative effect is more significant on the real interest rates of the LDCs than on those of the OECD countries.

Cross-sectional regression results show that the inflation rate is the only statistically significant economic instability indicator for both the LDCs and OECD countries. Although there are individual correlations between the volatility of the MRPK and inflation rate volatility, and real interest rate volatility, they are insignificant when entered into regressions together with the inflation rate.

The estimation results of the panel regressions provide that inflation rate is the most powerful force driving investment for low-inflation countries. Real exchange volatility affects investment decisions by itself, or in combination with inflation rate volatility. In high-inflation countries, inflation rate also affects investment decisions negatively. On the other hand, real exchange rate volatility has also negative and statistically significant effects on investment.

2.4 Real Exchange Rates, Volatility, and Investment

In Section 2.3, investment theories under certainty and uncertainty were explained, and empirical studies about investment under uncertainty were presented. In this section, the effects of real exchange rate changes and real exchange rate volatility on domestic and foreign investment decisions are discussed theoretically, and empirical studies are presented.

The real exchange rate is the price of foreign currency in terms of the domestic currency adjusted by the price differences between countries. The real exchange rate is an important determinant of the ex post facto return on internationally traded goods and many types of domestic goods.

The real exchange rate measures the price competitiveness of the domestic country relative to the foreign country. A real exchange rate depreciation decreases prices of domestic goods relative to prices of foreign goods. So, both domestic and foreign demand increase for domestic goods. This demand increase leads to expanded investment in exporting and import-competing industries.

Conversely, a real exchange rate appreciation increases domestic prices relative to foreign prices, so foreign demand for domestic goods decreases and domestic demand for foreign goods increases. This demand decrease leads to a contraction in investment in exporting and import-competing industries.[9]

Yet, as pointed out in Goldberg (1993), if production depends heavily on the imported intermediate materials (that is, import-oriented industries), and there are no domestic import-substitute materials, a depreciation of the domestic currency increases the cost of production. In this case, the net effect of depreciation on investment is ambiguous and depends on the relative weights of the export and import shares of production.

Real exchange rate changes cause reallocation of resources among the sectors. A depreciation of domestic currency may cause the reallocation of resources from the nontradable sector to the tradable sector (if substitutability exists between the sectors).

Real exchange rate changes also redistribute wealth across countries (Froot and Stein, 1991). A depreciation of domestic currency increases the wealth of foreign country relative to the that of domestic country. As a result, the weight of foreign preferences increases, and the weight of domestic preferences decreases. For instance, a depreciation of the U.S. dollar against the German mark increases the wealth of Germans relative to the wealth of Americans. Then, if Germans have strong preferences for the U.S. assets, German investment in the United States increases. However, if Germans have strong preferences for German assets, German investment in the United States decreases, and domestic investment in Germany increases.

On the other hand, real exchange rate volatility has negative effects on investment decisions. Real exchange rate volatility induces the transfer of resources from the tradable sector to the nontradable sector. It should be noted that the reallocation of resources among the sectors creates adjustment costs. Therefore, reallocation is realized only if the producers perceive that the exchange rate fluctuations are permanent (Batiz and Batiz, 1994; IMF, 1984). Short-term fluctuations may not affect the reallocation of the resources.

Real exchange rate volatility causes relocation of resources between countries (Goldberg and Kolstad, 1993; Aizenman, 1992). An uncertain exchange rate environment or high production costs induce firms to produce in a stable and cheaper country. This is the reason for the birth of multinational companies. With production location diversification, the production costs are decreased.

Aizenman (1992) analyzed the effects of exchange rate manipulation on domestic and foreign investments in the context of short-run expectations-augmented Phillips curves. In such a case, only unanticipated monetary shocks can affect the economy, so the exchange rate manipulation can impact domestic and foreign capital outflows. Aizenman's paper is unique, because it examines the effects of monetary and productivity shocks on the investment in the fixed and flexible exchange rate systems. Assuming agents are risk-neutral, Aizenman showed that both domestic and foreign investment are higher in a fixed exchange rate system, under both productivity and monetary shocks.

High real exchange rate volatility creates an uncertain environment for investment decisions. In an uncertain environment, investors delay their investment decisions to obtain more information about the real exchange rates if investments are irreversible (Pindyck, 1991; Engel and Hakkio, 1993; IMF 1984).

Large exchange rate shocks can cause "hysteresis" in trade if investments are irreversible (Dixit, 1989, 1992; Baldwin and Krugman,1989; Baldwin, 1988). When domestic currency appreciates, foreign firms enter the domestic market. Nevertheless, they do not abandon the domestic market when domestic currency depreciates, if they have sunk costs. Therefore, large exchange rate shocks can have persistent real effects by altering the structure of the domestic market, and thereby have a negative impact on the domestic investment decisions. Baldwin (1988) points out that small exchange rate shocks cannot have persistent real effects.

2.4.1 Empirical Studies About Real Exchange Rates, Volatility, and Investment

There are empirical studies that examine the effects of real exchange rates and real exchange rate volatility on investment expenditures. Pindyck and Solimano (1993) examined the effects of real exchange rate volatility, as well as the effects of other volatility measures on aggregate investment. Their study was presented in Section 2.3.2.

Campa and Goldberg (1995) and Goldberg(1993) examined the effects of real exchange rates and real exchange rate volatility on investment in the U.S. industries.

Luehrman (1991) explored the relation between the real exchange rates and investment of the firms in the auto and steel industries of the G-7 countries (that is, France, Germany, Italy, Japan, Sweden, United Kingdom, and United States)

Froot and Stein (1991) examined wealth effects of the real exchange rate changes on the foreign direct investment inflows into the United States as well as into the United Kingdom, Germany, Japan, and Canada.

Goldberg and Kolstad (1993) examined the relocation of resources between the U.S. and the United Kingdom, Japan, and Canada due to real exchange rate volatility.

In *Goldberg (1993)*, the effects of real exchange rate movements on U.S. industry were examined for the period 1970:1 to 1989:4. The objective was to determine how aggregate investment, as well as sectoral investment, respond to changes in real exchange rate levels and volatility.

Assuming investment is an increasing function of the expected profitability of a sector, the following regression equation is estimated for aggregate investment categories (that is, all industries, manufacturing, durable goods manufacturing, nondurable goods manufacturing, and nonmanufacturing industries) and their two-digit standard industrial classification (SIC) disaggregated sectors for the full sample period and two sub-periods (1970:1 to 1979:3 and 1979:4 to 1989:4).

$$I^i_t = a^i + b^i ER_t + c^i q_t + d^i GDP_t + e^i r_t + v_t$$

where,

I_t = investment in sector i at time t (that is, investment in new plants and equipment reported in constant dollars)

ER_t = real exchange rate

q_t = real exchange rate volatility

GDP_t = real Gross Domestic Product

r_t = ten-year U.S. Treasury bill rate

v_t = disturbance term

All the variables, except interest rates, are in logarithmic form. It is expected that in sector i, the sensitivity of investment to the real exchange levels and volatility is sector-specific.

Goldberg finds that real exchange rate levels and volatility have no statistically significant effect on aggregate investment in U.S. industry for the full sample. When the sample period is broken down, real exchange rate changes show statistically significant effects on the investment in durable goods manufacturing and nonmanufacturing sectors, but not in nondurable goods manufacturing sectors.

Real exchange rate changes had more significant effects on the investment in U.S. industry in the 1980s than in the 1970s. Contrary to theory, real U.S. dollar depreciations (appreciations) caused investment contractions (expansions) in the durable goods manufacturing and nonmanufacturing sectors during the 1980s. The contractionary effect of the depreciation can be caused by either the dominance of wealth effect or reliance on imported-intermediate goods.

When the industries are disaggregated into the two-digit SIC levels, it is observed that in the durable goods manufacturing sectors, real exchange rate volatility expanded investment in the 1970s and contracted investment in the 1980s. The investment contractions due to real exchange rate volatility can be explained by the risk-averse firm, irreversible investment, and profit convexity when imperfect competition exists. Finally, it is concluded that real exchange rate volatility does not have a large depressing effect on investment in U.S. industry.

Goldberg (1993) found that the depreciation of the U.S. dollar led to investment contractions in the U.S. industries during the 1980s, which is contrary to theory that depreciation should expand investment. *In her later study with Campa (1995)*, the patterns of external exposure through exports or imported inputs into production are analyzed. These patterns are used to examine the link between the exchange rate movements and domestic investment in the United States.

If the industry depends heavily on the imported inputs, a depreciation of domestic currency should depress investment. If the industry is highly export-oriented, a depreciation of domestic currency should expand investment. The net effect of the real exchange rate changes depends on the competitive structure of the industry. While oligopolistic (high markup) industries absorb the exchange rate changes, competitive (low markup) industries cannot.

Campa and Goldberg (1995) constructed the Index of Effective Exposure (IEE) to analyze whether the sectors are net importers or net exporters. Price-cost markup (PCM) ratios were calculated to decide the extent of the exchange rate pass-through, and the following regression equation is estimated by the Ordinary Least Squares (OLS) and Two Stages Least Squares (TSLS) techniques for 20 two-digit SIC manufacturing sectors from the years 1972 to 1986.

$$I_t / I_{t-1} = B_0 + B_1 \ (y_{t-1} \ /y_{t-2}) + (B_2 + B_3 p_t) \ e_{t-1} /e_{t-2} + (B_4 + B_5 p_t)$$
$$q_{t-1} \ / \ q_{t-2} \ + B_6 r_t \ / r_{t-1} \ + u_t$$

where

I_t	=	domestic investment in new plants and equipment in the manufacturing sector
y_t	=	industry sales
e_t	=	real exchange rate of the dollar against a trade weighted basket of currencies
q_t	=	real exchange rate volatility
r_t	=	ten-year U.S. treasury notes
p_t	=	industry external exposure that represents export shares of the industry, the imported input shares of the industry, the IEE of the industry, and industry markup ratios
u_t	=	error term

Real exchange rate volatility is estimated by two different variables. One is the ratio of the standard deviation to the mean of the exchange rate index over the previous twelve quarters. The other is the standard deviation of the first differences of the logarithm of the exchange rate over the twelve previous quarters.

The estimation results show that in the 1980s most of the U.S. manufacturing sectors became net importers. The share of imported inputs increased in production without any reduction in the export share. The U.S. dollar appreciations in the 1980s caused investment expansions in high markup sectors and investment contractions in low markup sectors. This shows that oligopolistic sector absorbs exchange rate movements rather than passing them to the prices.

Overall, the study concludes that real exchange rate volatility has weak and statistically insignificant effects on investment in the U.S. manufacturing industry.

Luehrman (1991) examined the relationship between real exchange rates and international price competitiveness of firms. He linked changes in competitiveness with redistribution of value within the world's automobile and steel industries during different periods between 1978 and 1987.

This study makes two contributions to the literature. First, firm-level competitiveness is used, which is consistent with the value maximizing behavior. Competitiveness is regarded as the firm's ability to get scarce cash flows. Second, data from the financial markets is used in the empirical part rather than from the product markets. The changes in the value of shares are computed from financial market data by assuming an integrated efficient world capital market, so the law of one price must hold for firm values. So, changes in the value shares of the firms caused by an exchange rate shock are compared.

It is assumed that cash flows are contestable. All of a firm's value comes from the scarce future cash flows, and the firm has to compete for these cash flows. Industry is defined as

> the set of scarce cash flows associated with a particular market. If cash flows were not scarce, competition would not be necessary. If they were not contestable, competition would not be possible.[10]

If world market is efficient, and if firms compete for the scarce product cash flows, a real home currency depreciation increases the value of the domestic firms relative to foreign competitors. In other words, the home country firms' share value should rise if cheapness makes them more competitive.

This hypothesis is tested by the following regression equation:

$$\ln (Y_{i,\,t+1} / Y_{i,t}) = a + b \, (\ln (S_{t+1} / S_t)) + u_t \qquad (1)$$

where

$Y_{i,t+1} / Y_{i,t}$ = change in share value of firm i in the industry.
S_{t+1} / S_t = changes in the value of domestic currency
u_t = error term

The null hypothesis b < 0 is tested against the alternative hypothesis b > 0. A rejection of the null hypothesis means that the test supports the theory (that is, b > 0). If the test fails (that is, b < 0), either there is a negative effect or the violations of the assumption that cash flows are not contestable.

If all the cash flows are not contestable, there will be changes in the share values that are not related to competitiveness. In this case, the industry definition and competitiveness criterion are not valid anymore, and translation effects due to translating between currencies are created. As a results, the estimation results will be biased.

Translation effects are subtracted from the firm's share value in the industry. Translation effect is the change in value share that would be observed from an exchange rate shock if all of a firm's value was denominated in its home currency, $(Y^{*i} = k^{*i}/S/ k^*_i /S)$ and k^*_i is equal to the local currency firm value for each firm and is obtained by local currency sample mean for each firm's value).

Then the revised model is as follows:

$$\ln(Y_{i,t+1}/Y_{i,t}) - \ln(Y^*_{i,t+1}/Y^*_{i,t}) = c + d\,(\ln S_{t+1} / S_t) + u_t \qquad (2)$$

The null hypothesis d > 0 is tested against the alternative hypothesis d < 0. If the null hypothesis is rejected, it means that a home currency depreciation causes a decline in a domestic firm's competitiveness.

These two hypotheses are tested using daily (May 2, 1985, through February 28, 1986), and weekly data (1985 through 1986, 1981 through 1982, and 1978 through 1979).

To test the hypotheses, the automobile and steel industries are selected. The reason for this selection is that these industries are most affected by real exchange rate changes, and have a large fraction of contestable cash flows. The steel industry includes 33 producers from the United States (18 firms), Japan (11 firms), and Germany (4 firms). The automobile industry includes 20 automobile producers from the United States (4 firms), Japan (6 firms), Germany (4 firms), France (1 firms), Italy (1 firm), Sweden (2 firms), and the United Kingdom (2 firms). The data used in the study are described as follows:

A firm's value equals the sum of its liabilities and equity. Value share of the firm is equal to the sum of its liabilities and equity in the U.S. dollars. Firms' values are computed in terms of local currencies, then in accordance with the law of one price translated into U.S. dollars.

Liabilities are included at their book values in local currency excluding pension/severance liabilities, untaxed special reserves (in Japan and Sweden), and minority interests in consolidated subsidiaries. Book values are from each company's most recent audited annual statement. Data on each firm's liabilities by fiscal year are from Daiwa Securities Analyst's Guide, Moody's International Manual, Moody's Industrial Manual, and each company's annual report. Equity value is the product of share prices and the number of shares outstanding for all classes of shares. Preferred stock issues, in which market prices are unavailable, are treated as liabilities denominated in the dividend currency and included at book value.

Daily stock prices are the closing prices in local currency from each firm's home equity market as quoted in the Financial Times, The Daily Stock Price Record, and the Asian Wall Street Journal. Weekly stock prices are the end of week prices from CRSP and from Interactive Data Corporation's Exshare database.

Daily exchange rates are spot prices of the U.S. dollar, at the middle of the bid-ask spread in each domestic market, from the International Financial Statistics of the International Monetary Fund. Weekly exchange rates are the middle of the spot bid-ask spread at the end of each week. The Japanese yen rates are from the Nikkei Telecom Japan News and Retrieval database. All rates for the European currencies are London quotes from Chase Manhattan Bank through the Interactive Data Corporation.

The estimation results do not support the theory that an exogenous real exchange rate depreciation enhances competitiveness of the domestic country vis-à-vis the foreign country. Conversely, a real exchange rate depreciation cause a decline in the relative value of home currency. The estimation results give strong rejection for the auto industry between 1985 to 1986 and 1981 to 1982, and for the steel industry between 1985 to 1986. During these periods, relative firm values are positively related to the value of the home currency. This may be caused by the wealth effects of the real exchange rate appreciations.

Froot and Stein (1991) examined the link between exchange rates and foreign direct investment (FDI) in an imperfect capital market. Imperfection comes from the asymmetric information about the asset's payoffs. The authors developed a model that can explain the effects of the exchange rate changes on foreign investment with asymmetric information. Asymmetry is ex post de facto, which is described as

> Once the profit from an asset is realized, it is costlessly seen only by the asset's owners. External creditors must pay an amount c if they want to observe the profit. This monitoring cost is what causes external finance to be more expensive than internal finance.[11]

In this model, agents are risk-neutral, and wealth increases stimulate the demand for foreign investment. If there is a link between wealth and investment, this link creates a relationship between exchange rate changes and FDI. It is also noted that, if there is no asymmetric information, there is no relationship between exchange rates and FDI. In this framework, domestic currency depreciation against foreign currency increases the wealth of foreign country residents relative to that of the domestic country residents. So, other things being equal, foreign country residents can buy more assets including domestic assets.

Froot and Stein (1991) compare the response of the FDI inflows to the exchange rates with that of other forms of foreign capital inflow into the United States from the period 1973 to 1988. Total foreign capital inflows include foreign official inflows and foreign private inflows. The foreign private inflows are also divided into three sub-categories: direct investment; U.S. treasury securities; corporate stocks and bonds, and other bonds. These foreign capital inflows are expressed in percentage of the U.S. gross national product

(GNP), and regressed on the real exchange rate and time trend. The regressions are estimated using both annual and quarterly time-series data.

Next, the U.S. FDI inflows are disaggregated into thirteen industries (that is, all industries, petroleum, manufacturing, food, chemicals, fabricated metals, machinery, other manufacturing, trade, finance, insurance, real estate, other industries). The data about the foreign capital inflows are from the Balance of Payments accounts.

Further, foreign capital inflows are disaggregated by the types of transactions (that is, all types, mergers and acquisitions, equity increases, real estate, new plant, joint ventures, plant expansion, other expansion, and no type listed). The foreign capital inflows are measured by both the value of transactions (that is, percentage of the U.S. GNP), and the number of transactions. The data is taken from the International Trade Administration.

Finally, the response of the U.S. FDI inflows with respect to exchange rate changes is compared with that of the FDI inflows into the United Kingdom, West Germany, Canada, and Japan between the years 1977 and 1987. The FDI inflows of the countries are taken from the Balance of Payments and expressed in percentage of the each country's GNP.

The estimation results show that FDI is the only capital inflow, that is negatively and statistically correlated with the value of the U.S. dollar by using both quarterly and annual data. When the U.S. dollar appreciates, FDI inflows into the United States decrease. There is a negative relationship between the real exchange rates and FDI inflows into the industries, and this relationship is significant for 5 industries. The most significant exchange rate effect is seen in the manufacturing industry, especially in the chemicals sectors.

There is also a negative relationship between both value, and the numbers of the transactions and real exchange rates. Mergers and acquisitions, which constitute 51 percent of the total foreign capital inflows into the United States in 1987, have also negatively significant coefficients for both value and numbers of the transactions.

At the country level, all the FDI inflows are negatively correlated with the real exchange rates, but the real exchange rate coefficients are only statistically significant for the United States and Germany.

As a conclusion, the empirical results provides that real exchange rates have some explanatory power on the foreign capital inflows, but they are not strong enough to explain all foreign capital inflows.

Goldberg and Kolstad (1993) explored the connection between the real exchange rate volatility and FDI flows, assuming firms are risk-averse and faced with revenue and cost uncertainty. Real exchange rate volatility is expected to increase the share of investment located in foreign countries. If the firms are risk-neutral, however, this share is not affected by real exchange rate volatility or other volatility measures.

The hypothesis is tested for the two-way bilateral foreign direct investment flows between the United States and the United Kingdom, Japan, and Canada. The data are quarterly from 1978:1 to 1991:4.

The regression equation is as follows:

$$(FDI / I) = a + b\, q_{e,t} + c\, q_{d,t} + d\, p_t + f\, e_t + g\, y_t + v_t$$

where

FDI / I	=	share of FDI outflow to the aggregate investment of source country
$q_{e,t}$	=	volatility of the bilateral real exchange rate
$q_{d,t}$	=	volatility of the real destination market demand
p_t	=	correlation between the real exchange rate and the real destination market demand
e_t	=	real exchange rate
y_t	=	real destination market demand (that is, real GDP)
v_t	=	disturbance term

The estimation results show that real exchange rate volatility has a positive sign, and is statistically significant for four of the six series of the bilateral FDI shares. Real exchange rate volatility increases investment share located in the foreign countries as expected in the theory. The real exchange rate coefficients have negative signs in all regressions, but they are not statistically significant. The real exchange rate depreciations make foreign investment expensive. As a result, investment outflows decreases that is consistent with the wealth effects. As explained in Section 2.4, page. 23, a depreciation of domestic currency decreases wealth of domestic country relative to that of the foreign country. So, domestic residents invest abroad less.

Until now, the effects of real exchange rate changes and real exchange rate volatility on domestic and foreign investment expenditures were examined theoretically and empirically.

To summarize; I can say that the empirical studies showed that both real exchange rate changes and real exchange rate volatility have explanatory power on real investment expenditures. But this explanatory power is very small or statistically insignificant depending upon assumptions made about environment. In the next section, I will discuss the results and implications of empirical studies.

2.5 Conclusion

After the collapse of the Bretton Woods fixed exchange rate system in March 1973, Australia, Canada, Finland, Japan, Norway, the United Kingdom, and the United States adopted a flexible exchange rate system. Some European countries adopted a quasi-fixed exchange rate system called the Exchange Rate Mechanism (ERM) of the European Monetary System (EMS) in March 1979.

According to the ERM of the EMS, every participating currency has a central rate expressed in terms of the European Currency Unit (ECU), and they cannot diverge from their ECU central rates beyond the margins of + / - 2.25 percent. The ECU is the basket of weighted member currencies. When currencies do deviate from their margins, their ECU shares are redefined by realignments, and revaluation (or devaluation) of the currencies are determined in order to eliminate changes in the relative prices. The ERM provides that the member currencies are fixed within the system, but flexible against the non-EMS currencies.

The ERM originally included Belgium, Denmark, France, Germany, Ireland, Italy, Luxembourg, and the Netherlands. However, Italy had wider exchange rate margins + / - 6 percent until January 1990. One of the main reasons for the establishment of the ERM was to create a stable exchange rate environment, and thereby induce investment and trade in Europe (Grauwe and Verfaille, 1988; Hilderbrandt, 1991). As explained by Engel and Hakkio (1993), the ERM introduces a new type of exchange rate volatility, volatility caused by the expectations of the realignments. When the realignment becomes inevitable, exchange rate volatility increases, but, volatility in this system is smaller as compared to that in the flexible exchange rate system.

On the other hand, no empirical study has been done about the effects of real exchange rate volatility on investment in the fixed versus flexible exchange rate systems. Hence, it is not possible to make any conclusion about the success of the ERM in this area.

Theoretically, real exchange rate changes and real exchange rate volatility can have important effects on real investment. Changes in the real exchange rate levels affect the international price competitiveness of the countries. This causes reallocation of resources among the sectors. Changes in the real exchange rate levels redistribute wealth across the countries.

Real exchange rate volatility causes reallocation of resources among the sectors, relocation of resources across countries, and creates an uncertain environment for investment decisions if investments are irreversible, thereby less investment is realized.

The volatility of the exchange rates influences the choice of international monetary systems. The negative implications of exchange rate volatility were the main reason for inception of the ERM of the EMS. Furthermore, recently, it is argued that exchange rates are too volatile; so the United States, Japan, and Germany should abandon the flexible exchange rate system and adopt a fixed exchange rate system like the ERM of the EMS (Engel and Hakkio, 1993; Frankel and Meese, 1987).

All these arguments imply that exchange rate volatility has depressing effects on domestic and foreign investment decisions of firms, and these effects can be reduced or eliminated by adoption of a fixed exchange rate system.

Empirical studies investigated the effects of both real exchange rate changes and real exchange rate volatility on investment decisions in various ways. The studies show that real exchange rates and real exchange rate volatility have explanatory power on national and foreign direct investment decisions. However, it is empirically showed that, this explanatory power is very small or statistically insignificant depending upon assumptions made about environment.

For instance, Pindyck and Solimano (1993) concluded that only inflation rate has negative and statistically significant effects on investment using aggregated investment data pooled across countries. Since they used pooled aggregate investment data, this may mask different patterns at the sectoral level. For instance, exporting sectors are likely to react differently than the importing sectors to changes in exchange rates.

Campa and Goldberg (1995) and Goldberg (1993) addressed this issue by using investment data at the sectoral level. These studies also resulted that real exchange rate volatility has no depressing effects on investment in U.S. industry. But, they used only U.S data. The United States is large, and has a relatively closed economy whose businesses historically are not oriented to international markets. Therefore, the response of investment decisions to exchange rate levels and volatility may not be high.

Moreover, Goldberg (1993) proved that the U.S. dollar appreciations (depreciations) caused investment expansions (contractions) in the U.S. durable goods manufacturing and nonmanufacturing industries in the 1980s, which was contrary to theory. This result implies that real exchange rates misjudge the effects of the real exchange rate changes on investment unless export and import exposure of the sectors are considered.

Therefore, further study should examine both the effects of real exchange rate changes and real exchange rate volatility on investment at the sectoral level for open economies. Theoretically, the effects of the real exchange rates on investment are analyzed more precisely when the export and import exposure of the sectors are measured. Hubbard (1994) describes the advantages of using sectoral level investment data as follows:

For researchers and practitioners interested in empirical applications and potential policy implications, however, the lessons of the new view would be more compelling if couched in *industry equilibrium.* This is because most firms constantly struggle with the prospect of competition in investment from other incumbents and potential entrants. The concept of irreversibility is also perhaps more appropriately analyzed at the industry level because the liquidity of most assets in place is surely greater within than outside the industry.[12]

As explained by Artis and Taylor (1994), volatility can be transferred from exchange rates to interest rates. A reduction in the real exchange rate volatility may cause an increase in real interest rate volatility. Real interest rate volatility is another source of uncertainty and as explained in Ingersoll and Ross (1992), real interest rate uncertainty has depressing effects on investment decisions. For that reason, the effects of real interest rate volatility in addition to real exchange rate volatility should be examined to determine if there is a volatility transfer from exchange rates to interest rates.

NOTES

1.   John Maynard Keynes, *The General Theory of Employment, Interest, and Money* (San Diego: Harcourt Brace Jovanovich, 1936), p. 135.

2.   Duesenbery (1958), Knox (1952), and Tinbergen(1938) describe the model in detail.

3.   More detailed information about the Neoclassical theory is contained in Abel (1991), Branson and Litvack (1986), Hall and Jorgenson (1971), and Jorgenson (1963, 1967).

4.   Robert S. Pindyck, "Irreversibility, Uncertainty, and Investment." *Journal of Economic Literature*, September 1991, Vol. XXIX, p. 1141.

5.   Robert S. Pindyck, "Irreversibility, Uncertainty, and Investment." *Journal of Economic Literature*, September 1991, Vol. XXIX, p. 1112.

6.   Baldwin and Krugman (1989) and Dixit (1989a) describe hysteresis in trade in detail.

7.   Robert S. Pindyck, "Irreversibility, Uncertainty, and Investment." *Journal of Economic Literature*, September 1991, Vol. XXIX, p. 1142.

8.   Brownian motion is the random walk in the continuous time. Brownian motion is explained in Section 3.2, p. 43.

9.   Richardson (1988) examines changes in the U.S. auto competitiveness relative to Japanese auto firms by comparing the trends in effective exchange rates and relative auto prices from 1979 to 1985. The results show that a decrease in the U.S. auto prices relative to Japanese auto prices, which means U.S. auto competitiveness increases.

10.   Timothy A. Luehrman, "Exchange Rate Changes and the Distribution of Industry Value." *Journal of International Business Studies*, 1991, 21, p. 621.

11. Kenneth A. Froot and Jeremy C. Stein, "Exchange Rates and Foreign Direct Investment: An Imperfect Capital Market Approach." *Quarterly Journal of Economics,* November 1991, 106 (94), p. 1196.

12.   R. Glen Hubbard, "Investment Under Uncertainty: Keeping One's Options Open." *Journal of Economic Literature,* December 1994, Vol. XXXII, p.1825.

III

Methodology

3.1 Introduction

In this chapter, the effects of the real exchange rate uncertainty on the investment decisions of firms are analyzed using option pricing techniques, and then the regression equations to be estimated, excluding and including sector-specific foreign trade data, in the empirical part of the study in Chapters 5 and 6 are presented. Accordingly a detailed description of variables are reported.

The procedure of this chapter is as follows:

In Section 3.2, the value of the investment project and value of the firm's option to invest and optimal stopping point under real exchange rate uncertainty are determined for export-oriented and import-competing firms, as well as import-oriented firms using option pricing techniques. It is assumed that present real exchange rate volatility is a proxy for future real exchange rate uncertainty, and investment spending is like a call option in the finance literature. When investment is realized, it kills the option to invest. Therefore, investment decisions of the firms will be sensitive to real exchange rate uncertainty.

In Section 3.3, the investment equations to be estimated in the empirical part of the study in Chapters 5 and 6, and a detailed description of the variables are presented.

In Section 3.4, the construction of variables including sector-specific foreign trade data, which will be used in Chapter 6, are presented.

3.2 The Effects of Real Exchange Rate Uncertainty on the Investment Decision

In this section, the value of an investment project, and the value of a firm's option to invest under real exchange rate uncertainty are analyzed using option pricing techniques.

The objective is to show that real exchange rate volatility depresses real investment spending in either export-oriented and import-competing firms or import-oriented firms. *Present real exchange rate volatility is a proxy to future real exchange rate uncertainty.* These examples are similar to Pindyck (1991), pp. 1125-1132.

Most of the sectoral investments are sector-specific, hence, they cannot be used in another sector efficiently. The feature of sector specifity of investment spending makes them irreversible. As explained by Pindyck (1991), the investment spending can be delayed for further information about real exchange rates.

Accordingly, the characteristics of irreversibility and ability to delay investment spending for further information make investment decisions of firms more sensitive to real exchange rate uncertainty.

The *real exchange rate*, that is, e, is the price of the foreign currency in terms of the domestic currency adjusted by the ratio of foreign prices to domestic prices. The real exchange rate measures the price competitiveness of domestic firms relative to foreign firms. An increase in the real exchange rate (that is, depreciation of domestic currency) implies that price competitiveness of domestic firms increases relative to the foreign firms, and vice versa.

According to the purchasing power parity (PPP) doctrine, real exchange rates are equal to a constant in the long run, and changes in the nominal exchange rates tend to equalize relative price changes. Therefore, real exchange rate follows a *mean-reverting stochastic process* (Krugman, 1989; Dixit, 1989a). Such a process can be represented by

$$de = \alpha (\mu - e) dt + \sigma e^v dz \qquad (3.1)$$

where *de* is the changes in real exchange rate, α is the speed of adjustment parameter, μ is the long run equilibrium real exchange rate, *dt* is the time interval, σ is the volatility of the real exchange rate, and *dz* is an increment of a Brownian motion (or Wiener process). *The Brownian motion* is the random walk in the continuous time. The increments of a Brownian motion are independent regardless of the size of the time interval. Using of Brownian motion gives an opportunity to think a firm's entry and exit decisions as options depending on real exchange rate volatility. Hence, we can apply option pricing techniques.

The increment of a Brownian motion can be represented as $dz = \varepsilon(t)\, dt^{1/2}$, where $\varepsilon(t)$ is a serially uncorrelated, $E(e_t\, e_k) = 0$ for $t \neq k$, and normally distributed random variable with mean *zero* and standard deviation *1*, and *dt* is the changes in time. Accordingly, if E denotes the expectations operator, $E(dz) = 0$ and $E(dz)^2 = dt$.

Empirically, the speed of adjustment to PPP has been found to be very slow, so PPP only holds in the very long run. Frankel and Meese (1987) find that the speed of adjustment to PPP is sufficiently low such that rejecting zero speed of adjustment is statistically impossible. For that reason, the speed of adjustment parameter α is set to zero. In this way, the effects of the real exchange rates on investment decisions are excluded from the analysis, while, the effects of real exchange rate volatility are the focus.

The parameter v is set to 1 to obtain an analytical solution to the resulting differential equations. This analysis illustrates the effects of real exchange rate volatility on the investment decisions of firms. The procedure is similar to Dixit (1989, 1992), Krugman (1989), and Pindyck (1991). Thus, equation (3.1) is now

$$de = \sigma e\, dz \qquad (3.2)$$

hence, the square of equation (3.2) is

$$de^2 = \sigma^2\, e^2\, dt \qquad (3.3)$$

3.2.1   Export-Oriented and Import-Competing Firms

In this part, it is assumed that the firm is a risk-neutral exporting or import-competing firm. The objective is to show that, when real exchange rate volatility increases, the firm will wait for a higher real exchange rate level to occur before undertaking the investment project.

First, the value of the project, that is, the plant, will be calculated. I assume that the plant itself can be considered as having an option either to produce or shut-down depending on the level of the real exchange rates. I assume that it can be reopened without cost, since this simplifying assumption does not change the conclusions here.

Once the value of the plant is derived, then I calculate the value of the option to undertake investment in the plant or wait.

Then, the *optimal stopping point*, that is, the level of the real exchange rate at which it is optimal to undertake investment, is obtained.

Finally, I show the effects of real exchange rate volatility on the optimal stopping point.

3.2.1.1 Value of the Plant Under Real Exchange Rate Uncertainty

The value of the plant depends on its current and expected cash flows. Here the cash flow is simplified to a linear function of the real exchange rate relative to some break-even real exchange rate, that is, $\bar{e}$. The *break-even real exchange rate* is the real exchange rate at which the firm's cash flows are positive. Then, as indicated by equation (3.4), if the real exchange rate is greater than the break-even rate, the sum of the expected capital gain from an investment and expected cash flows (or operating profits) must be equal to the risk-free return on an investment of equivalent value.

If the real exchange rate is less than the break-even rate, the plant is shut down to avoid negative cash flows. Although there are no cash flows, the investment still has value because of the option to reopen. In this case, changes in the value of the investment, that is, the expected capital gain in the plant's value, is set equal to the risk-free return (that is, equation (3.5)). Thus

$$r\,V(e)\,dt \;=\; E\,(dV) \,+\, \gamma(e-\bar{e}\,) \qquad\qquad \textit{if } e > \bar{e} \qquad (3.4)$$

$$r\,V(e)\,dt \;=\; E\,(dV) \qquad\qquad\qquad\qquad \textit{if } e < \bar{e} \qquad (3.5)$$

where e is the real exchange rate, $\bar{e}$ is the break-even real exchange rate, $V(e)$ is the present value of the investment, r is the risk-free interest rate, dt is the time interval, $E(dV)$ is the expected capital gains from the investment, and $\gamma\,(e - \bar{e}\,)$ is the expected cash flows from the investment.

These two equations are solved separately subject to boundary conditions (3.6) through (3.9).

$$V\,(0) \;=\; 0 \qquad\qquad\qquad e < \bar{e} \qquad (3.6)$$

$$V_e(\bar{e}-) \;=\; V_e(\bar{e}+) \qquad\qquad e = \bar{e} \qquad (3.7)$$

$$V(\bar{e}-) \;=\; V(\bar{e}+) \qquad\qquad e = \bar{e} \qquad (3.8)$$

$$\lim_{e\to\infty} V\,(e) \;=\; \gamma\,\frac{(e-\bar{e})}{r} \qquad\qquad e > \bar{e} \qquad (3.9)$$

These boundary conditions are used to identify the function of V, in addition to the differential equations implied by (3.4) and (3.5).

Equation (3.6) states that if the real exchange rate is equal to zero, it remains zero. Therefore, the plant has no value.

Equations (3.7) and (3.8) state that the value of the plant is a continuous and smooth function of the real exchange rate at $\bar{e}$.

Equation (3.9) states that if the real exchange rate is excessively large, there is no possibility that the plant will stop producing. Therefore, the plant is similar to a perpetuity, and its return is measured by $\gamma\,(e - \bar{e}\,)\,/\,r$.

First, equation (3.4) is evaluated. Ito's Lemma[1] is used to express

$$dV = V_e \, de + \frac{1}{2} V_{ee} \, de^2 \qquad (3.10)$$

where $V_e = dV / de$ and $V_{ee} = d^2V / de^2$. Substituting equation (3.2) for de and equation (3.3) for de^2 in equation (3.10) gives

$$dV = V_e \, (\sigma e dz) + \frac{1}{2} V_{ee} \, (\sigma^2 e^2 dt) \qquad (3.11)$$

The expectations of both sides of equation (3.11) are taken. Since $E[dz] = 0$, the following equality is obtained

$$E \, (dV) = \frac{1}{2} V_{ee} \, \sigma^2 \, e^2 dt \qquad (3.12)$$

Therefore, equation (3.4) can be written as

$$rVdt = \frac{1}{2} V_{ee} \, \sigma^2 \, e^2 dt + \gamma(e - \bar{e})dt \qquad (3.13)$$

Simplifying and rearranging equation (3.13) yields an ordinary differential equation that $V(e)$ must satisfy

$$\frac{\sigma^2}{2} e^2 \, V_{ee} - rV + \gamma e - \gamma \bar{e} = 0 \qquad (3.14)$$

The proposed solution to this ordinary differential equation is as follows:

$$A_1 e^{\beta_1} + A_2 e + A_3 = V \qquad (3.15)$$

Taking the second derivative of (3.15) with respect to e and putting it into equation (3.14) yields $A_2 = \gamma / r$ and $A_3 = -\gamma \bar{e} / r$. Then the value of the plant, $V(e)$, is

$$V(e) = A_1 e^{\beta_1} + \gamma \left[\frac{e - \bar{e}}{r} \right] \qquad e > \bar{e} \qquad (3.16)$$

where $(\sigma^2/2) [\beta_1 (\beta_1 - 1)] - r = 0$. This is a quadratic equation and the roots are either $\beta_1 < 0$, or $\beta_1 > 1$. Boundary condition (3.9) indicates that as e approaches infinity, the value of the plant, that is, V, is like a perpetuity discounted by interest rate r, and the value of option to shut down, that is, $A_1 e^{\beta_1}$, approaches 0. Therefore, it must be true that $\beta_1 < 0$.

Next, equation (3.5) is evaluated, which is repeated here for convenience.

$$rVdt = E\,(dV) \qquad e < \bar{e} \qquad (3.17)$$

and

$$rVdt = \frac{\sigma^2}{2} V_{ee}\, e^2\, dt \qquad e < \bar{e} \qquad (3.18)$$

Rearranging equation (3.18) yields the following differential equation

$$\frac{\sigma^2}{2} e^2\, V_{ee} - rV = 0 \qquad e < \bar{e} \qquad (3.19)$$

Again, V must satisfy this ordinary differential equation. The proposed solution is given as

$$A_4 e^{\beta_2} = V \qquad (3.20)$$

Taking the second derivative of equation (3.20) with respect to e, and substituting into equation (3.19) gives

$$\left[\frac{\sigma^2}{2}\beta_2(\beta_2 - 1) - r\right] A_4 e^{\beta_2} = 0 \qquad (3.21)$$

This quadratic equation is the same as that obtained in (3.16). Since (3.20) must meet the boundary condition (3.6), so, it must be true that $\beta_2 > 1$. The coefficients of (3.16) and (3.20), that is, A_1 and A_4, are found by using the boundary conditions (3.7) and (3.8). These boundary conditions yield the following equations respectively.

$$A_1 e^{-\beta_1} + \gamma \frac{(\bar{e} - \bar{e})}{r} = A_4 e^{-\beta_2} \qquad (3.22)$$

$$\beta_1 A_1 e^{-(\beta_1 \cdot 1)} + \frac{\gamma}{r} = \beta_2 A_4 e^{-(\beta_2 \cdot 1)} \qquad (3.23)$$

The value of the plant is as

$$V(e) = \frac{\gamma}{r} \frac{e^{-(1-\beta_1)}}{(\beta_2 - \beta_1)} e^{\beta_1} + \frac{\gamma}{r}(e - \bar{e}) \qquad e > \bar{e} \qquad (3.24a)$$

$$V(e) = \frac{\gamma}{r} \frac{e^{-(1-\beta_2)}}{(\beta_2 - \beta_1)} e^{\beta_2} \qquad e < \bar{e} \qquad (3.24b)$$

Equations (3.24a) and (3.24b) can be explained intuitively as follows:
When $e > \bar{e}$, the plant is operating and continues to operate regardless of the changes in the real exchange rates. The present value of the future operating profits is equal to $\gamma (e - \bar{e}) / r$, which is the second term on the right-hand side, and the value of the plant's option to close is the first term on the right-hand side.
When $e < \bar{e}$, the plant is not producing. In this case, equation (3.24b) is the value of the option to reopen in the future. It should be noted that the value of the plant is not equal to zero when $e < \bar{e}$ because of the value of the option to reopen, unless $e = 0$, because $e = 0$ is an absorbing barrier.

3.2.1.2 The Value of Option to Invest in the Plant and Optimal Stopping Point

The value of the firm's option to invest in the plant is a function of the value of the plant, which is a function of the real exchange rate. Hence, let $F(V(e)) = F(e)$ be the value of the option to invest in the plant. Assume the option to invest is exercised at the optimal stopping point, that is, e^*, otherwise it is optimal to wait. In this case, $F(e^*)$ must satisfy the following boundary conditions:

$$F(0) = 0 \qquad (3.25)$$

$$F(e^*) = V(e^*) - I \qquad (3.26)$$

$$F_e(e^*) = V_e(e^*) \qquad (3.27)$$

Equation (3.25) states that, if the real exchange rate is equal to zero, the real exchange rate stays at zero; hence, the value of the option to invest in a valueless plant is zero.

Equation (3.26) states that when investment is made, the firm receives a net payoff $V(e^*) - I$, where I is the cost of building the plant (that is, sunk cost).

Equation (3.27) is *the smooth pasting condition*. At this point, it is not worthwhile to wait for a higher real exchange rate to occur because the value of the option to invest and the plant's value are increasing at the same rate.

Assume a firm is waiting for the new information about the real exchange rates. While waiting to build, there are no cash flows. Therefore, expected capital gains on the opportunity to invest are equal to the risk-free return on an investment of equivalent value, that is

$$rFdt = E(dF) \qquad (3.28)$$

By using Ito's Lemma, dF is expressed as

$$dF = F_e \, de + \frac{1}{2} \, F_{ee} \, de^2 \qquad (3.29)$$

Substituting equation (3.2) for de and equation (3.3) for de^2 in equation (3.29) yields the following equation

$$dF = F_e \, (\sigma e dz) + \frac{1}{2} \, F_{ee} \, (\sigma^2 e^2 dt) \qquad (3.30)$$

Taking expectations of equation (3.30) yields the following equation

$$E(dF) = \frac{1}{2} \, \sigma^2 \, e^2 \, F_{ee} \, dt \qquad (3.31)$$

Replacing $E(dF)$ in equation (3.28) with equation (3.31) and cancelling dts gives

$$rF - \frac{1}{2} \, \sigma^2 \, e^2 \, F_{ee} = 0 \qquad (3.32)$$

Equation (3.32) is an ordinary differential equation which is solved subject to the boundary conditions (3.25), (3.26), and (3.27). The proposed solution to (3.32) is given by

$$F(e^*) = ae^{\beta_3} \quad for \quad e < e^* \qquad (3.33)$$

Taking the second derivative of equation (3.33) with respect to e, and substituting into equation (3.32) yields the following equation

$$\left[\frac{\sigma^2}{2} \, \beta_3 \, (\beta_3 - 1) - r \right] a \, e^{\beta_3} = 0 \qquad (3.34)$$

This quadratic equation is the same as equation (3.21). Therefore, either $\beta_3 = \beta_2$, or $\beta_3 = \beta_1$. Boundary condition $F(0) = 0$ implies that $\beta_3 > 0$. Hence, $\beta_3 = \beta_2$.

Finally, the value of e^* and coefficient a are determined using the boundary conditions (3.26) and (3.27). At the optimal stopping point, e^*, these boundary conditions must be satisfied. These boundary conditions yields

$$\frac{\gamma}{r}\frac{\bar{e}^{-(1-\beta_1)}}{(\beta_2\,\beta_1)}\, e^{*\,\beta_1}\,\frac{\gamma}{r}\,(e^* - \bar{e}) - I = a\,e^{*\,\beta_2} \tag{3.35}$$

$$\beta_1\,\frac{\gamma}{r}\frac{\bar{e}^{-(1-\beta_1)}}{(\beta_2-\beta_1)} + \frac{\gamma}{r} = \beta_2\,a\,e^{*\,(\beta_2-1)} \tag{3.36}$$

The coefficient a is determined from (3.36). It is

$$a = \frac{\gamma}{r}\left[\frac{\beta_1}{\beta_2}\frac{\bar{e}^{-(1-\beta_1)}}{(\beta_2-\beta_1)}\,e^{*(\beta_1-\beta_2)} + \frac{e^{*\,(1-\beta_2)}}{\beta_2}\right] \tag{3.37}$$

Substituting (3.37) into equation (3.35) gives the equation that e^* must satisfy, which is

$$\frac{\bar{e}^{-(1-\beta_1)}}{(\beta_2-\beta_1)}\left(1-\frac{\beta_1}{\beta_2}\right)e^{*\,\beta_1} + \left(1-\frac{1}{\beta_2}\right)e^* - \left(\bar{e}+\frac{rI}{\gamma}\right) = 0 \tag{3.38}$$

The real exchange rate e^* is the "*optimal stopping point*". Intuitively, this is the point at which the real exchange rate is high enough to induce the firm to build the plant, rather than wait for the real exchange rate to move higher. Hence, the relationship between the volatility of real exchange rates and the optimal stopping point, e^*, is determined. This answers the question, "*Does the volatility raise the optimal stopping point?*"

If volatility raises the optimal stopping point, then volatility increases the zone at which it is optimal to wait, rather than invest. Since an increase in volatility raises individual $e*$ on all investment projects, thus widening the zone in which it is optimal to wait rather than invest, aggregate investment in each sector will decrease for a given real exchange rate level. Hence, real exchange rate volatility lowers real investment spending, other things being equal.

Defining (3.38) as Φ, I will show that

$$\frac{de^*}{d\sigma^2} = -\frac{\Phi_{\sigma^2}}{\Phi_{e^*}} > 0 \tag{3.39}$$

where Φ_{σ}^2 and Φ_{e^*} are the derivatives of function Φ with respect to σ^2 and $e*$. This inequality indicates that an increase in real exchange rate volatility increases the real exchange rate that initiates the investment. Φ_{e^*} is

$$\Phi_e{}^* = \left(\frac{1}{\beta_2}\right)\left[\beta_1\left(\frac{\bar{e}}{e^*}\right)^{(1-\beta_1)} + \beta_2 - 1\right] \tag{3.40}$$

The definitions of roots, $\beta_1 = 1/2 - 1/2\,(1 + 8r/\sigma^2)$ and $\beta_2 = 1/2 + 1/2\,(1+8r/\sigma^2)$ and the fact that $\bar{e} \leq e* \leq \infty$, $e*$ will not go below the break-even point imply that (3.40) is non-negative. Φ_{σ}^2 is

$$\Phi_{\sigma^2} = \Phi_{\beta_1}\frac{d\beta_1}{d\sigma^2} + \Phi_{\beta_2}\frac{d\beta_2}{d\sigma^2} \tag{3.41}$$

which is

$$\Phi_{\sigma^2} = c\left(\frac{e^*}{\beta_2}\right)\left[\left(\frac{e^*}{\bar{e}}\right)^{(\beta_2-1)}\left(\ln\left(\frac{e^*}{\bar{e}}\right) - \frac{1}{\beta_2}\left(1 - \left(\frac{e^*}{\bar{e}}\right)^{(\beta_1-1)}\right)\right)\right] \tag{3.42}$$

where $c = 2r / (\sigma^2)^2 [1 + 8r / \sigma^2]^{-1/2}$. Inspection of (3.42) shows that it is zero when $e* = 0$ and negative when $e*$ approaches infinity. Therefore, I determine that Φ_σ^2 is negative. Take the first derivative of (3.42) with respect to $e*$ to determine whether there is maxima (or minima). A negative value of (3.42) at the optima will indicate Φ_σ^2 is negative over the range of $\bar{e} \leq e* \leq \infty$. Taking the derivative of (3.42) with respect to $e*$ and then solving for $e*$ gives

$$\ln \left(\frac{e^*}{\bar{e}} \right) = - \left[\frac{1}{\beta_2} + \frac{1}{\beta_1 - 1} \right] \tag{3.43}$$

Substituting equation (3.43) into equation (3.42) and making necessary cancellations gives

$$\Phi_{\sigma^2} = -c \left(\frac{e^*}{\beta_2} \right) \left[\left(\frac{e^*}{\bar{e}} \right)^{(\beta_1 - 1)} \left(\frac{1}{\beta_1 - 1} \right) - \frac{1}{\beta_2} \right] \tag{3.44}$$

It was demonstrated earlier that $\beta_1 < 0$ and $\beta_2 > 1$; moreover, it was argued that $(e* / \bar{e}) \geq 1$. Using these facts and the values of β_1 and β_2 defined by the quadratic equation in (3.16) and (3.20), one can show that $\Phi_\sigma^2 < 0$. Thus, since Φ_σ^2 is continuous and is equal to zero at $e* = \bar{e}$, and negative as $e*$ approaches infinity, it is negative at its only *extremum*. Therefore, $\Phi_\sigma^2 < 0$.

Since $\Phi e* > 0$ and $\Phi \sigma^2 < 0$, then $-\Phi \sigma^2 / \Phi e* > 0$. Hence, $de*/d\sigma^2 > 0$. All else held equal, the uncertainty measured by the volatility of the real exchange rates increases the optimal stopping point, implying lower investment spending.

3.2.2 Import-Oriented Firms

In this part, it is assumed that plants are import-oriented. In other words, their production depends heavily on imported materials. The real exchange rate represents the cost of imported materials. Then the value of the plant and value of the option to invest in the plant under real exchange rate uncertainty are analyzed.

In this part, it is shown that the optimal stopping point, e^*, at which it is optimal to invest in the plant, is lower than it otherwise would have been, when real exchange rate volatility increases. This increases the zone where it is optimal to wait rather than invest. When aggregated across firms in the sector, this implies that investment spending is negatively related to real exchange rate volatility, other thing being equal.

3.2.2.1 Value of the Plant Under Real Exchange Rate Uncertainty

Again, the plant's value depends on the relative magnitudes of the real exchange rate and break-even real exchange rate. If real exchange rate is less than the break-even rate, the plant is producing because cash flows are positive. So, the sum of the expected capital gain from an investment and expected cash flows (or operating profits) must be equal to the risk-free return on an investment of equivalent value.

If the real exchange rate is greater than the break-even rate, the plant is closed to avoid negative cash flows. The return on the plant is its cash value and its capital gain, that is, the change in its value, which includes the value of the option to reopen. Now,

$$r\,V(e)\,dt = E\,(dV) + \lambda(\bar{e} - e)\,dt \qquad if\ e < \bar{e} \qquad (3.45)$$

$$r\,V(e)\,dt = E\,(dV) \qquad if\ e > \bar{e} \qquad (3.46)$$

which are analogous to equations (3.4) and (3.5) in the case of exporting firms described in Section 3.2.1.1. The boundary conditions are also similar to boundary conditions (3.6) through (3.9) in Section 3.2.1.1 for the export-oriented and import-competing firms. In this case, they are

$$V(0) = 0 \qquad\qquad e > \bar{e} \qquad\qquad (3.47)$$

$$V(\bar{e}-) = V(\bar{e}+) \qquad\qquad e = \bar{e} \qquad\qquad (3.48)$$

$$V_e(\bar{e}-) = V_e(\bar{e}+) \qquad\qquad e = \bar{e} \qquad\qquad (3.49)$$

$$\lim_{e \to 0} V(e) = \lambda \frac{(\bar{e} - e)}{r} \qquad\qquad e < \bar{e} \qquad\qquad (3.50)$$

Equation (3.47) states that when the real exchange rate equals zero, it remains zero, and the plant has no value.

Equations (3.48) and (3.49) state that the value of the investment is a continuous and smooth function of the real exchange rate at the break-even point, $\bar{e}$.

Equation (3.50) states that if the real exchange rate is extremely small, there is no possibility that the firm will stop producing, so the plant's cash flows are measured by $\lambda (\bar{e} - e) / r$, and the value of the option to reopen approaches zero.

The value of the plant is determined analogously to the case for the exporting and import-competing firms in Section 3.2.1.1 (see Appendix A.1 for derivations). The value of the project is

$$V(e) = \frac{\lambda}{r} \frac{e^{-(1-\alpha_1)}}{(\alpha_1 - \alpha_2)} e^{\alpha_1} + \frac{\lambda}{r} (\bar{e} - e) \qquad e < \bar{e}$$

$$(3.51.)$$

$$V(e) = \frac{\lambda}{r} \frac{e^{-(1-\alpha_2)}}{(\alpha_1 - \alpha_2)} e^{\alpha_2} \qquad\qquad e > \bar{e}$$

where $\alpha_2 < 0$ and $\alpha_1 > 0$.

When $e < \bar{e}$, the plant is operating and continues to operate regardless of the changes in the real exchange rates. The present value of the future operating profits is equal to $\lambda (\bar{e} - e) / r$, and the value of the firm's option to close will be the first part of the first equation.

When $e > \bar{e}$, the plant is not producing. In this, case the value of the option to reopen in the future is equal to equation (3.51).

3.2.2.2 The Value of Option to Invest in the Plant and Optimal Stopping Point

The value of the option to invest under real exchange rate uncertainty for the import-oriented firms is $F(V(e)) = F(e)$. Assume the firm makes an investment at the optimal stopping point, $e*$, which is less than $\bar{e}$; otherwise the firm waits. In this case, $F(e*)$ must satisfy

$$\lim_{e \to \infty} F(0) = 0 \qquad (3.52)$$

$$F(e^*) = V(e^*) - I \qquad (3.53)$$

$$F_e(e^*) = V_e(e^*) \qquad (3.54)$$

Equation (3.52) states that if the real exchange rate goes to infinity, option to invest goes to zero.

Equations (3.53) and (3.54) are similar to equations (3.26) and (3.27) in Section 3.2.1.2 for the export-oriented and import-competing firms.

Equation (3.53) states that the option to invest is exercised when $0 < e* < \bar{e}$. When investment is realized, the firm receives a net payoff $V(e^*) - I$, where I is the cost of building the plant.

Equations (3.54) is *the smooth pasting condition*. At this point, it is not worthwhile to wait for a lower real exchange rate to occur, because the value of the option to invest and the value of plant are increasing at the same rate.

Similar manipulations to those in Section 3.2.1.2 yield an equation that $e*$ must fulfill (see Appendix A.2 for derivations).

$$\frac{\lambda}{r} \frac{e^{-(1-\alpha_1)}}{(\alpha_1-\alpha_2)} \left(1-\frac{\alpha_1}{\alpha_2}\right) e^{*\alpha_1} + \frac{\lambda}{r} \left(\frac{1}{\alpha_2}-1\right) e^* + \frac{\lambda}{r}\bar{e} - I = 0 \quad (3.55)$$

Finally, the relationship between the volatility and the optimal stopping point, $e*$, is determined. What effect does a volatility increase have on $e*$? Letting Ψ equal (3.55), it is shown that

$$\frac{de^*}{d\sigma^2} = -\frac{\Psi_{\sigma^2}}{\Psi_{e^*}} < 0 \quad (3.56)$$

where Ψ_{σ^2} is the derivative of the implicit function with respect to σ^2 and Ψ_{e^*} is the derivative of the implicit function with respect to $e*$.

In Appendix (A.2), it is shown that $-\Psi_{\sigma^2} / \Psi_{e^*} < 0$, and therefore $de* / d\sigma^2 < 0$. This result proves that the optimal stopping point, $e*$, decreases when volatility is higher, and an increase in the real exchange rates depresses real investment spending, and vice versa.

To summarize, real exchange rate uncertainty proxied by present real exchange rate volatility causes optimal stopping point, $e*$, to be higher for export-oriented sectors and lower for import-oriented sectors. Thus the zone of *"inaction"* increases, and real investment spending falls as volatility increases regardless of whether the sector is an export-oriented or import-oriented sector.

3.3 Estimation Equations and Description of the Variables

This section presents the regression equations to be estimated in the empirical part of the study, and provides a detailed descriptions of the variables. Differences between this study and Pindyck and Solimano (1993) and Goldberg (1993) are also discussed.

Pindyck and Solimano (1993) examine the effects of real exchange rate volatility, as well as inflation rate and inflation rate volatility on the aggregate investment of six low- (that is, France, Germany, Japan, the Netherlands, the United Kingdom, the United States) and six high-inflation (that is, Argentina, Bolivia, Brazil, Chile, Israel, Mexico) countries using panel data pooled across countries. Data are annual and cover the period 1960 to 1990. In the regression equation, the dependent variable is the ratio of real investment to real GDP. Investment is measured by the total and private investments taken from the national records. Explanatory variables are real exchange rate volatility, inflation rate, inflation rate volatility, lag of the growth rate of the real GDP, and lag of the dependent variable.

Goldberg (1993) explores the effects of real exchange rates and real exchange rate volatility on the U.S. aggregate investment categories (that is, all industries, manufacturing, durable goods manufacturing, nondurable goods manufacturing, and non manufacturing industries) and their two-digit SIC disaggregated sectors using quarterly time-series data from the period 1970:1 to 1979:4, and two sub-periods (1970:1 to 1979:3 and 1979:3 to 1989:4). Investment is measured by the investment in new machinery and equipment in constant dollars. Explanatory variables are the real exchange rate, real exchange rate volatility, real GDP, and real interest rate.

In this study, three specifications are estimated. Since there are two dependent variables, that is, total investment in fixed assets and investment in machinery and equipment, six regressions are estimated. The data are annual from 1979 to 1993 and pooled across sectors within each country. Data at the two-digit and, if available, the three-digit international standard industrial classification (ISIC) manufacturing sectors, are used. The three specifications are:

(1) $I / VA_{i,t} = a_0 + a_1 ER_{i,t} + a_2 ERV_{i,t} + a_3 R_{i,t} + a_4 RV_{i,t} +$

$a_5 INF_{i,t} + a_6 INFV_{i,t} + a_7 OP_{i, t-1} + a_8 GGDP_{i, t-1} +$

$a_9 GVA_{i, t-1} + a_{10} (I / VA)_{i,t-1} + a_{11} T_{i,t} + a_{12} SQ_{i,t} + u_{i,t}$

(2) $I / VA_{i,t} = b_0 + b_1 ER_{i,t} + b_2 ERV_{i,t} + b_3 R_{i,t} + b_4 RV_{i,t} +$

$b_5 INF_{i,t} + b_6 OP_{i, t-1} + b_7 GGDP_{i, t-1} + b_8 GVA_{i, t-1}$

$+ b_9 (I / VA)_{i,t-1} + b_{10} T_{i,t} + b_{11} SQ_{i,t} + u_{i,t}$

(3) $I / VA_{i,t} = c_0 + c_1 ER_{i,t} + c_2 ERV_{i,t} + c_3 R_{i,t} + c_4 RV_{i,t} +$

$c_5 OP_{i, t-1} + c_6 GGDP_{i, t-1} + c_7 GVA_{i, t-1} +$

$c_8 (I / VA)_{i,t-1} + c_9 T_{i,t} + c_{10} SQ_{i,t} + u_{i,t}$

where,

$(I / VA)_{i,t}$	=	ratio of investment to value added for sector i in year t
$ER_{i,t}$	=	real exchange rate
$ERV_{i,t}$	=	real exchange rate volatility
$R_{i,t}$	=	real interest rate
$RV_{i,t}$	=	real interest rate volatility
$INF_{i,t}$		inflation rate
$INFV_{i,t}$	=	inflation rate volatility
$OP_{i, t-1}$	=	openness of the economy to the international markets in year t-1
$GGDP_{i, t-1}$	=	growth rate of the real GDP in year t-1
$GVA_{i, t-1}$	=	growth rate of value added for sector i in year t-1
$(I / VA)_{i, t-1}$	=	the dependent variable in year t-1
$T_{i,t}$	=	time trend
$SQ_{i,t}$	=	time trend squared
$u_{i,t}$	=	disturbance term

It is assumed that the response of sectoral investment to the real exchange rates and real exchange rate volatility is sector-specific.

The dependent variable is the ratio of investment to value added. Investment is measured by total investment and investment in machinery and equipment. Both investments and value added are at the sectoral level.

The independent variables are described as follows:

The real exchange rate is the price of the foreign currency in terms of the domestic currency adjusted by the price differences between countries. A real exchange rate depreciation decreases prices of domestic goods relative to prices foreign goods, so both foreign and domestic demand increase for domestic goods. This demand increase leads to expanded investment in exporting and import-competing sectors.

A real exchange rate appreciation increases domestic prices relative to foreign prices, so foreign demand for domestic goods decreases, and domestic demand for foreign goods increases. This demand decrease leads to a contraction in investment in exporting and import-competing industries.

However, if an industry depends heavily on the imported materials, and there are no domestic import-substitute materials, a depreciation should contract investment and an appreciation should expand investment. Hence, it is better to test this hypothesis with the framework of disaggregated export and import data, rather than aggregated data. The sign of the coefficient is expected to be negative. If the sector depends heavily on imported materials, the sign of the coefficient is expected to be positive.

Real exchange rate volatility is a measure of real exchange rate uncertainty. According to Sections 3.2.1.2 and 3.2.2.2, since real investments are irreversible, real exchange rate volatility creates an uncertain environment, which causes investors to delay their investment decisions to obtain more information about the real exchange rates. Thus, real exchange rate uncertainty depresses investment. The sign of the coefficient is expected to be negative.

The real interest rate measures the cost of capital and is a proxy for the user cost of capital. The user cost of capital is a function of prices of investment goods, real interest rate, and depreciation rate. If we assume depreciation rate is fixed, real interest rate is used as a proxy to the user cost of capital. An increase in user cost of capital depresses investment spending. According to traditional investment theory (that is, the Neoclassical theory), if real interest rates are high, it will be costly to borrow funds for investment and, therefore, the sign of the coefficient is expected to be negative.

Pindyck and Solimano (1993) and Ingersoll and Ross (1992) show that higher real interest rates may increase investment in the short run by reducing the incentive to wait for future information. In the same way, a reduction in real interest rates may not increase investment because the cost of waiting is lowered. Therefore, the sign of the coefficient is ambiguous and an empirical issue.

Real interest rate volatility is a measure of real interest rate uncertainty. As explained in Ingersoll and Ross (1992), real interest rate uncertainty reduces the optimal acceptance level of interest rates that initiates the investment. Since investments are irreversible, the firm finds it optimal to wait to invest until a higher interest rate is reached. As a result, investment decreases, other things being equal. The sign of the coefficient is expected to be negative.

The inflation rate is the rate of change in general price level. Inflation may have detrimental effects on investment spending. As explained in Wilson (1982), in an inflationary environment, not all the prices rise, nor do they rise to the same extent. Therefore, relative prices are distorted, and resources are reallocated from productive investments to unproductive investments, such as housing, real estate, inventories, etc.

High inflation also discourages new productive investments due to difficulty in predicting future costs and profits. Fischer and Modigliani (1978) state that high inflation increases uncertainty about future price levels. Consequently, high inflation causes productivity slowdown. Wilson (1982) notes that high production costs (that is, money wages, material costs, resource costs) can be transmitted to prices quickly. Therefore, productivity may decrease in order to compensate increases in the production costs.

Conversely, it is also argued that a moderate inflation may increase investment (Odeh, 1968). A small increase in output prices stimulates producers to increase production and capacity. For instance, Odeh (1968) found a positive relationship between the inflation rate and gross private investment in Brazil. Pindyck and Solimano (1993) also mention that in Mexico in the 1970s, transition from low inflation to moderate inflation occurred along with a corresponding increase in investment rates, which was mostly due to public investment. Thus, also in regard to inflation, the sign of the coefficient is ambiguous and an empirical issue.

Inflation rate volatility measures inflation rate uncertainty. Inflation rate uncertainty creates an uncertain environment about future production costs, as well as real output prices and, therefore, firm's revenues. Hence, if investments are irreversible, firms can delay investment decisions to wait for a more stable inflationary environment. The sign of the coefficient is expected to be negative.

Openness of the economy to the international markets improves productivity through specialization. However, if international trade mostly includes importing goods, investment may decrease when openness of the economy increases, so again the sign of the coefficient is ambiguous and an empirical issue. Levine and Renelt (1992) find a positive robust relationship between the investment share of GDP and international trade share of GDP. They also show that this result does not change, if they replace the total international trade only with exports or imports. The lag of the variable used in the estimation.

The growth rate of the real GDP measures overall demand variables in the economy. According to the accelerator-principle theory, investment is a linear function of the changes in output. An increase in the real GDP increases investment. Since investment decisions are made depending on the past values, lag of the growth rate of the real GDP is used in the estimation. The sign of the coefficient is expected to be positive.

The growth rate of value added measures the profitability of an individual sector. An increase in output stimulates investment. Since there is a time lag between the investment decisions are made and the investments are actually realized, the lag of the growth rate of value added is used in the estimation. The sign of the coefficient is expected to be positive.

The lag of the dependent variable measures existing capital stock. According to the Neoclassical theory, investment demand is a function of the difference between the desired capital stock and the actual capital stock. It takes time to realize last year's desired capital stock, so the sign of the coefficient is expected to be positive.

3.4 Description of the Variables Including Sector-Specific Foreign Trade Data

As mentioned in the Introduction, sector level foreign trade data are available for the countries of Finland, Germany, the United Kingdom, and the United States. Therefore, the effects of the export and import exposure of individual sectors on their investment decisions are analyzed separately in Chapter 6.

Regressions which do not include the export or import share of the sectors may underestimate the effects of real exchange rates and real exchange rate volatility on investment decisions. Interaction variables defined by these shares multiplied by the real exchange rates are included in a separate set of regression estimates for these countries and reported in Chapter 6.

It is expected that these estimates may be even stronger than those obtained without this data, since Goldberg (1993) showed that the results obtained without these interaction variables led to incorrect results. Specifically, these additional variables are defined as follows:

The export exposure of the sector is measured by the ratio of exports to production interacted by real exchange rates. This variable measures export exposure of the sector. An appreciation of the real exchange rate decreases investment spending when the export share of sector rises. The sign of the coefficient is expected to be negative.

The import exposure of the sector is measured by the ratio of imports to production interacted by real exchange rates. This variable measures import exposure of the sector. An appreciation of the real exchange rate increases investment when the import share of sector rises. The sign of the coefficient is expected to be positive.

The foreign trade exposure of the sector is measured by the ratio of exports plus imports to production multiplied by two-year real exchange rate volatility. This variable measures openness of the sector. The sign of the coefficient of this variable is expected to be negative based on the discussions in Sections 3.2.1.2 and 3.2.2.2.

NOTES

1. The Ito's lemma is as a Taylor series expansion. More detailed information about Ito's lemma is contained in Pindyck (1991), pp. 1144-1146 and Pindyck and Dixit (1994), pp. 79-82.

IV

Description of the Data

4.1 Introduction

Investment (gross fixed capital formation) in two- and three-digit international standard industrial classification (ISIC) disaggregated manufacturing sectors are used in the empirical part of the study.[1] Investment data consist of two series: total investment and investment in machinery and equipment. Data are cross-sectional (across sectors), annual time-series data from the years 1979 to 1993 for each country. Sectoral level data are collected by the Economic Analysis and Statistics Division of the Directorate for Science, Technology, and Industry of the Organization for Economic Cooperation and Development (OECD) Secretariat under the name of *"Industrial Structure Statistics."*

Other data sources were searched to find investment data in the manufacturing sectors (that is, International Financial Statistics of the International Monetary Fund, World Bank, Citibase, EUROSTAT). However, the OECD database is the only source that provides data for both EMS and non-EMS countries at the sectoral level classified according to ISIC.

This data source also provides sector-specific foreign trade data for Finland, Germany, the United Kingdom, and the United States. Foreign trade data gives the opportunity to analyze the effects of real exchange rates and real exchange rate volatility on real investment spending, while controlling for export and import exposure in each sector. To the best of my knowledge, this data source has not been used in any previous empirical investment study.

This chapter presents a detailed description of data and variables used in the empirical part of the study in Chapters 5 and 6.

In the second section, detailed information about data sources, data collection processes, and data definitions are reported.

In the third section, the construction of cross-sectional time-series data and the estimation technique are described.

In the fourth section, the types and construction of both the dependent and independent variables used in the regression equations in Chapters 5 and 6 are reported.

In the last section, the construction of variables, including sector-specific foreign trade data is reported.

4.2   Data Sources and Definitions

Investment for each sector is reported as total investment and investment in machinery and equipment. The OECD data are divided into two groups according to sources: data collected from the national industrial surveys and data from the national accounts disaggregated by sector.

Industrial surveys contain the results of the sample industrial surveys conducted by the national statistical organizations of the countries. There is no uniform sampling procedure for the surveys between the countries. Each country uses its own sampling procedure. Therefore, the percentage of the industry covered in the surveys may change from country to country. Some countries extrapolate data to account for the unsampled portion. Since the data are not collected uniformly across countries, data were not pooled across countries. Instead the data were pooled across sectors within each country.

The national accounts are disaggregated by sectors. Thus, national accounts use a "top-down" approach, while industrial surveys use a "bottom-up" approach. The countries used in this study, and their data sources, are listed as follows:

1. Belgium (National Accounts)
2. Denmark (Industrial Surveys)
3. Finland (Industrial Surveys)
4. France (National Accounts)
5. Germany (Industrial Surveys)
6. Italy (Industrial Surveys)
7. The Netherlands (Industrial Surveys)
8. Norway (National Accounts)
9. United Kingdom (Industrial Surveys)
10. United States (Industrial Surveys)

Total investment, or gross fixed capital formation, is defined as the value of purchases of fixed assets plus own-account construction, less the value of sales of fixed assets. Fixed assets (that is, land, buildings, plant, equipment) are the assets those have a productive life of at least one year, and include new assets (unused, or previously used outside the country), used assets, the assets produced by the unit's labor force for its own use, and additions, alterations, improvements, and repairs to existing assets. The valuation of the fixed assets is incurred at the full cost including transportation costs, installation costs, fees, and taxes.

Investment in machinery and equipment is defined as gross fixed capital formation in machinery and equipment, and has the same definition with that of the total investment. Investment in machinery and equipment includes investment in transportation equipment; industrial machinery and equipment; office machinery, equipment, and furniture; professional equipment and instruments. Alterations and improvements to these items are also included in the valuation.

The definition and valuation of fixed assets show differences in some countries. These differences are described as follows:

In Denmark, fixed assets are defined as those that have a productive life of at least three years.

In France, taxes and fees are excluded from the valuation of fixed assets.

In Germany and Italy, the value of sales are not deducted from the value of purchases.

In the Netherlands, the valuation of fixed assets includes indirect taxes, and excludes fees and VAT.

The United States does not report the purchases of used plant and equipment due to confidentiality. The data on the sales of fixed assets are not also collected. Therefore, total fixed assets include only new plant and equipment, and total investment is the expenditure on new plant and equipment. The valuation of new assets are at delivered prices including cost of installation, but excluding fees and taxes.

4.3   Description of Cross-Sectional Time-Series Data and Estimation Technique

The OECD investment data do not provide enough observations to estimate either a cross-sectional or time-series equation. Therefore, annual time-series data are pooled across sectors for each country separately. Pooling gives larger data sets to estimate regression equations.

Assume there are n cross-sectional sectors, $i = 1, 2, 3, \ldots .n$ at each time period T, $t = 1, 2, 3, 4, \ldots .T$. The total number of observations will be $n * T$. Greene $(1993)^2$ generalizes the cross-sectional time-series analysis by the following regression equation

$$Y_{it} = \alpha_i + \beta' X_{it} + \varepsilon_{it} \qquad (4.1)$$

where $E[\varepsilon_{it}] = 0 \qquad Var[\varepsilon_{it}] = \sigma^2$

In this equation there are K regressors in X_{it}, not including the constant term. The constant term, that is, α_i, measures the individual effects. Individual effects are specific to the individual cross-sectional sector i, and are constant over time t. Assume y_i and X_i are the T observations for the *ith* sector, and ε_i is $T * 1$ vector of disturbance matrix. Then (4.1) can be represented in matrix form as

$$
\begin{bmatrix} y_1 \\ y_2 \\ y_3 \\ \vdots \\ y_n \end{bmatrix} = \begin{bmatrix} \alpha_1 \\ \alpha_2 \\ \alpha_3 \\ \vdots \\ \alpha_n \end{bmatrix} + \begin{bmatrix} X_1 \\ X_2 \\ X_3 \\ \vdots \\ X_n \end{bmatrix} \beta + \begin{bmatrix} \varepsilon_1 \\ \varepsilon_2 \\ \varepsilon_3 \\ \vdots \\ \varepsilon_n \end{bmatrix} \tag{4.2}
$$

The *"Fixed-Effects"* model is chosen to estimate regression equations. In this way, *sector-specific factors* that affect the investment decisions can be captured by an intercept that varies among the sectors. By including the fixed effects equation (4.1) can be written as

$$
y_i = i\alpha_i + \beta X_i + \varepsilon_i \tag{4.3}
$$

Equation (4.3) can be represented in matrix form as

$$
\begin{bmatrix} y_1 \\ y_2 \\ y_3 \\ \vdots \\ y_n \end{bmatrix} = \begin{bmatrix} i\,0\,0.\ldots0 \\ 0\,i\,0.\ldots0 \\ 0\,0\,i.\ldots0 \\ \vdots \\ 0\,0\,0.\ldots i \end{bmatrix} + \begin{bmatrix} \alpha_1 \\ \alpha_2 \\ \alpha_3 \\ \vdots \\ \alpha_n \end{bmatrix} \begin{bmatrix} X_1 \\ X_2 \\ X_3 \\ \vdots \\ X_n \end{bmatrix} \beta + \begin{bmatrix} \varepsilon_1 \\ \varepsilon_2 \\ \varepsilon_3 \\ \vdots \\ \varepsilon_n \end{bmatrix} \tag{4.4}
$$

The size of this matrix is equal to $nT * n$. If d_i represents the dummy variable showing the *ith* sector, then the matrix form can be represented as

$$y = [d_1, d_2, \ldots .d_n \ x] \begin{bmatrix} \alpha \\ \beta \end{bmatrix} + \varepsilon \qquad (4.5)$$

This matrix representation can be expressed as a regression equation as follows:

$$y_i = \alpha_1 \ d_1 i + \alpha_2 \ d_2 i + \ldots .+ \alpha_i d_j + X_i \beta' + \varepsilon_i \qquad (4.6)$$

In equation (4.6), each α_i represents a sector-specific constant for the *ith* sector, and d_j is the sector-specific dummy variable for the *ith* sector. Sector-specific dummy variable d_j is equal to 1 when $i = j$. This regression model is called Least Squares Dummy Variable (LSDV) model and is estimated by using the Ordinary Least Squares (OLS) technique.

4.4 Definitions of the Variables

This section reports a detailed explanation of the variables included in the empirical part of the study in Chapters 5 and 6.

4.4.1 Dependent Variables

There are two dependent variables. The first one is the ratio of total investment in fixed assets to value added. The second one is the ratio of investment in machinery and equipment to value added. Both investment expenditures and value added are sector-specific and measured in national currencies.

It is well-known that most of the macroeconomic variables are non-stationary including investment. Since annual investment data are used for at most 14 years, this number of observations is not enough to test the time-series properties of the investment data. Accordingly, the ratio of investment to value added is used as a dependent variable. In this way, trend growth is eliminated. It should be noted that it is better to scale investment to capital stock, but, because of the unavailability of capital stock data for each sector and country, value added is used. The dependent variables are in logarithmic form.

4.4.2 Independent Variables

In this section, independent variables that are used in the regressions are explained in detail. The growth rate of the value added variable is sector-specific. All the other variables are the same for all sectors.

Real Exchange Rate is measured by the real effective exchange rate index compiled by the International Monetary Fund's (IMF) International Financial Statistics (IFS). The real effective exchange rate index is defined in terms of relative unit labor costs in the manufacturing industries and compares relative profitability of nonlabor factors in producing manufactured goods at home and abroad. Therefore, the real exchange rate tends to equalize the return on nonlabor factors across the industries.

The IFS computes the real effective exchange rate index as "the ratio (expressed on the base 1990 = 100) of an index of the period average exchange rate of the currency in question to a weighted geometric average of exchange rates for the currencies of selected partner or competitor countries adjusted for relative normalized unit labor costs in manufacturing."

The real effective exchange rate index is prepared only for industrialized countries using a single definition. This characteristic gives an opportunity to make a comparison across countries. Clark et al. (1994), in examining the different indicators of international price competitiveness, determined that the real effective exchange rate index defined in terms of the relative labor costs is the best measure of international price competitiveness of countries.

An increase in the real effective exchange rate index shows an appreciation of the domestic currency. Hence, the sign of the coefficient is expected to be negative for net exporting industries, and positive for net importing industries. The real exchange rate is in logarithmic form.

Expected Two-Year Real Exchange Rate Volatility is measured by the standard deviation of monthly real effective exchange rate indexes. Two measures were constructed. One used one year's worth of monthly data, the other used two years' worth of monthly data. Either could be a realistic interval over which firms use historical data to form expectations of future volatility.

According to Sections 3.2.1.2 and 3.2.2.2, since real investments are irreversible, real exchange rate volatility creates an uncertain environment that causes investors to delay their investment decisions to obtain more information about the real exchange rates. Therefore, the sign of the coefficient is expected to be negative.

Real Interest Rate is constructed from the nominal interest rate such as the long-term (that is, ten-year) government bond yield. The real interest rate is constructed by taking differences between long-term government bond yields and annual inflation rates. Due to the unavailability of long-term government bond yields for Finland, the average bank lending rate is used as a proxy for long-term nominal interest rates. Data are taken from the IFS database. Theory indicates that the sign of the coefficient is ambiguous. An increase in real interest rates reduces investment through raising the cost of capital. On the other hand, an increase in real interest rates raises investment in the short run by reducing the incentive to wait (Ingersoll and Ross, 1992).

Expected Real Interest Rate Volatility is measured by the standard deviation of the monthly real interest rates. Two proxies, one using one year's worth of monthly, and one using two years' worth of monthly historical data were constructed. Real interest rate uncertainty reduces the optimal acceptance level of interest rates that initiates investment. Since the investments are irreversible, the firm waits to invest until a higher interest rate is reached. Consequently, investment spending decreases. The sign of the coefficient is expected to be negative.

Annual Inflation Rate is measured by the mean of each year's monthly inflation rates. Monthly inflation rate is the percentage change in the Consumer Price Index (CPI). Data are taken from the IFS database. The CPI is chosen to measure inflation rate because of the availability of data on a monthly basis to calculate inflation rate volatility. Most theoretical studies indicate that the sign of the coefficient is expected to be negative (that is, Fischer and Modigliani, 1978; Wilson, 1982). On the other hand, Pindyck and Solimano (1993) and Odeh (1968) found a positive effect of inflation on investment. Hence, the sign of the coefficient is ambiguous and an empirical issue.

Expected Inflation Rate Volatility is measured by the standard deviation of the monthly inflation rates. Two proxies, one using one year's worth of monthly and one using two years' worth of monthly historical data were constructed. Inflation rate uncertainty creates an uncertain environment about future production costs as well as real output prices and, therefore, firms' revenues. If investments are irreversible, firms can delay investment decisions to wait for a stable inflationary environment. The sign of the coefficient is expected to be negative.

Openness of the economy is calculated by the ratio of exports plus imports to the GDP. Exports are the merchandise exports (that is, free on board (FOB)), and imports are the merchandise imports (that is, including the costs of insurance and freight (CIF)) from the international transactions reported by the IFS. The lag of the openness of the economy variable is used in the estimation. The sign of the coefficient is expected to be positive.

Growth rate of the real GDP is calculated as the percentage change in the real GDP. The real GDP is in 1990 prices and is taken from the IFS database. Since investment decisions are made depending on the past values, the lag of the growth rate of the real GDP is used in the estimation. The growth rate of the real GDP measures demand variables affected by the macroeconomic policies. Hence, the sign of the coefficient is expected to be positive.

Growth Rate of Value Added is measured by the percentage changes of sector-specific value added (that is, net output). Value added is the gross output less the cost of materials, fuels, and other supplies; contract expense and commissions; repair and maintenance work done by others; goods shipped in the same condition as received; and electricity purchased. The value added data are taken from the Industrial Structure Statistics of the OECD. The lag of the growth rate of value added is used in the estimation. Since the growth rate of value added measures the profitability of the individual sector, the sign of the coefficient is expected to be positive.

Time Trend measures the autonomous changes in investment. The autonomous changes are caused by technical changes and are independent of the explanatory variables. In the estimation, time trend and the square of the time trend are used.

4.4.3 Independent Variables Including Sector-Specific Foreign Trade Data

As mentioned in the Introduction, sector-specific foreign trade data are available for the countries of Finland, Germany, the United Kingdom, and the United States. Therefore, the effects of the export, import and foreign trade exposure of the sectors on investment decisions for these countries are analyzed separately in Chapter 6.

For these countries, in addition to variables described in Section 4.4.2, the following sector-specific variables are constructed and replaced with the real exchange rate and real exchange rate volatility in the investment equations.

Export Exposure of the sector is measured by the ratio of exports (FOB) to production multiplied by real exchange rate. Exports and production are sector-specific and in national currencies. Production is the gross value of production, including the value of all products, allowing for net change of work in progress, goods shipped in the same condition as received, net changes in stock levels of finished goods, services rendered and electricity sold. The valuation is in factor values, excluding all indirect taxes and including all subsidies. The production data are taken from the Industrial Structure Statistics of the OECD. The sign of the coefficient is expected to be negative.

Import Exposure of the sector is measured by the ratio of imports (CIF) to production multiplied by real exchange rate. Imports and production are sector-specific and in national currencies. The sign of the coefficient is expected to be positive.

Foreign Trade Exposure (that is, openness of the sector) is measured by the ratio of exports plus imports to production multiplied by real exchange rate volatility. All the data are sector-specific and in national currencies. The sign of the coefficient is expected to be negative.

NOTES

1. The ISIC codes and names of the two-digit manufacturing sectors are as follows:

31	Food, Beverages and Tobacco
32	Textile, Apparel and Leather
33	Wood products and Furniture
34	Paper, Paper Products and Painting
35	Chemical Products
36	Non-Metalic Mineral Products
37	Basic Metal Industries
38	Fabricated Metal Products
39	Other Manufacturing

The ISIC codes and names of the three- and four-digit manufacturing sectors are presented below. Four-digit manufacturing sectors are also included if they are available.

311.2	Food
313	Beverages
314	Tobacco
321	Textiles
3212	Knitting Mills
322	Wearing Apparel
323	Leather and Products
324	Footwear
331	Wood Products
332	Furniture and Fixtures
341	Paper and Products
3411	Pulp, Paper and Board
342	Printing and Publishing
351	Industrial Chemicals
3511	Basic Industrial Chemicals
3512	Fertilizers and Pesticides
3513	Synthetic Resins

352	Other Chemicals
3521	Paints, Varnishes and Lacquers
3522	Drugs and Medicines
3523	Soap and Cleaning Preparations
3529	Chemical Products
353	Petroleum Refineries
354	Petroleum and Coal Products
355	Rubber Products
356	Plastic Products
361	Pottery, Chine etc.
369	Non-Metalic Products
371	Iron and Steel
372	Non-Ferrous Metals
381	Metal Products
3813	Structural Metal Products
382	Non-Electrical Machinery
3821	Engines and Turbines
3822	Agricultural Machinery
3823	Metal and Wood Working Machinery
3824	Special Industrial Machinery
3825	Office and Computing Machinery
3829	Machinery and Equipment
383	Electrical Machinery
3831	Electrical Industrial Machinery
3832	Radio, TV and Communication Equipment
3833	Electrical Appliances and Housewares
3839	Electrical Apparatus
384	Transport Equipment
3841	Shipbuilding and Repairing
3842	Railroad Equipment
3843	Motor Vehicles
3844	Motorcycles and Bicycles
3845	Aircraft
3849	Transport Equipment
385	Professional Goods
3851	Professional Equipment
3852	Photographic and Optical Goods
3853	Watches and Clocks

2. More detailed information about cross-sectional time-series data is contained in Greene (1993), pp. 444-465.

V

Empirical Results and Implications

5.1 Introduction

In this chapter, the estimation results of the three investment equations described in Chapter 3 are analyzed. These equations are estimated for all examined countries. Since sector-specific foreign trade data are available for only four of these countries, the estimation of equations including these data were done in a separate step and are presented in Chapter 6.

The equations are estimated using the investment data in the manufacturing sectors by the Ordinary Least Squares (OLS) technique. Investment data are annual time-series data from the years 1979 to 1993.[1] Data are pooled across sectors within each country. The equations are estimated for total investment and investment in machinery and equipment in the manufacturing sectors separately. The sectors are broken down into two categories as two- and three-digit ISIC disaggregated manufacturing sectors.

The procedure of this chapter is as follows:

The overview of the estimation results and econometric issues related to estimation procedure are presented in the second section.

The estimation results for the countries in the ERM of the EMS are reported in the third section.

The estimation results for the countries in the flexible exchange rate system are reported in the fourth section.

The summary of the estimation results are presented in the last section.

5.2 Overview of the Estimation Results

The estimation results support the hypothesis that real exchange rate volatility has negative and statistically significant effects on real investment in the manufacturing sectors of the countries in the flexible exchange rate system. This negative significant effect is robust for both total investment and investment in machinery and equipment.

On the other hand, real exchange rate volatility has negatively significant effects on investment only in the German manufacturing sectors and has no statistically significant effects on investment in the manufacturing sectors of the rest of the EMS countries. Real exchange rate volatility coefficients are either statistically insignificant or positively significant in the regressions for the EMS countries.

In the EMS countries, the inflation rate and inflation rate volatility have more explanatory power on investment spending in the manufacturing sectors. Real interest rate volatility has negatively significant effects on investment in the Danish, French, and German manufacturing sectors.

Before discussing the estimation results for each country separately, some econometric issues related to the estimation procedure are addressed.

During the estimation procedure, sector-specific dummies are included into the equations to capture the sector-specific fixed effects.

The dependent variables and the real exchange rates are in logarithmic form, and all the other variables are in levels.

Both one- and two-year volatility measures are used in the estimation. However, the two-year volatility measure shows more significance than the one-year volatility measure; therefore, only the two-year volatility measure was used here.

Both the time trend and the square of the time trend are included in the regressions. They are retained in the regressions if they are statistically significant, otherwise they are dropped.

The current and lagged values of the real exchange rate, real interest rate, and inflation rate are used in the estimation, and the statistically significant ones retained in the regressions.

Heteroscedasticity (that is, disturbance terms have different variances) may be a problem if the pooled time-series do not have the same variances. In the presence of heteroscedasticity, the OLS estimation results are still unbiased, but inefficient. Heteroscedasticity makes the standard errors of the regression coefficients and their t-values inaccurate. Therefore, statistical significance tests of the coefficients are not valid. The White (1980) test was applied to test for the existence of heteroscedasticity. If the White (1980) test did not reject the existence of heteroscedasticity, the White heteroscedasticity correction was applied.

When the lagged dependent variable is included in a regression, the Durbin Watson statistic for autocorrelation test is not appropriate. For that reason, the serial correlation is tested by the Lagrange Multiplier (LM) serial correlation test up to the second order.[2] First order test results are reported in tables. Serial correlation was not detected in the estimations.

Another problem with the time-series data is the non-stationarity of the data. Although there are not enough observations to test the stationarity of the data, all the variables are expressed in a form that excludes the possibility of random walks on a theoretical basis. For instance, investment is scaled to value added, real exchange rate is in index form, etc.

5.3 Estimation Results for the Countries in the European Monetary System

In this section, the estimation results for the member countries of the ERM of the EMS are presented. The estimation results support the hypothesis that real exchange rate volatility has no depressing effects on investment in the manufacturing sectors. Real exchange rate volatility has depressing effects on investment only in the German manufacturing sectors.

Even though Germany is a member of the ERM of the EMS, the German mark is freely floating against the non-EMS currencies. Germany has a large open economy, and much German trade is with non-EMS countries. Therefore, real exchange rate volatility may have depressing effects on investment expenditures. Real exchange rate volatility has positive and statistically significant effects on investment in the Netherlands' manufacturing sectors. Real interest rate volatility has depressing effects on investment in France, Germany, and Denmark. Real interest rate volatility has positive effects on investment in Belgium and statistically insignificant effects on investment in the Netherlands.

On the other hand, inflation rate volatility has depressing effects on sectoral investment in France and Italy. The inflation rate has depressing effects on investment in Belgium, Germany, and the Netherlands.

5.3.1 Estimation Results for Belgium

The estimation results for the Belgium two- and three-digit manufacturing sectors are reported in Tables 5.1 and 5.2 respectively. The estimation period covers the periods 1980 to 1992 for total investment, and 1983 to 1992 for investment in machinery and equipment.

The estimation results do not support the hypothesis that real exchange rate volatility has depressing effects on investment in the manufacturing sectors, but do support the hypothesis that real exchange rate volatility depresses investment in machinery and equipment. While, real exchange rate volatility coefficients are statistically insignificant in the regressions using total investment data, they are negatively significant in the regressions using investment in machinery and equipment data.

Real interest rate volatility coefficients are positively significant in the regressions together with inflation rate and inflation rate volatility. This result shows that real interest rate volatility causes investment expansions contrary to theory. The inflation rate volatility coefficients are negatively significant in the regressions except for the total investment in two-digit manufacturing sectors. It should also be noted that real exchange rate volatility and real interest rate volatility coefficients are only statistically significant in the regressions together with inflation rate and inflation rate volatility. When inflation variables are dropped from the regressions, adjusted R squared values do not change or changes a little. This indicates that there is inverse collinearity between the variables. In this case, none of the regressions show strong evidence that volatility matters.

In most of the cases, the coefficients of other variables have the expected positive or negative values. The real exchange rate coefficients are statistically significant only in equation (3) using total investment and in equation (2) using investment in machinery and equipment data at the two-digit level. This shows that real exchange rate appreciation has positive effects on investment spending. The real interest rate coefficients are negatively significant in the regressions as expected. The inflation rate coefficients are negatively significant in the regressions as expected.

The variable that measures openness of the economy to the international markets has positively significant coefficients in equations (1) and (2) using investment in machinery and equipment data. They are statistically insignificant in the other regressions. The coefficients of the growth rate of the real GDP are positively significant in equations (1) and (2) using three-digit level total investment data and in equation (1) using two-digit level investment in machinery and equipment data. In the other regressions the coefficients of the growth rate of the real GDP are either statistically insignificant or negatively significant, which is contrary to the expected values. The coefficients of the growth rate of value added are statistically insignificant in all regressions, which is contrary to the expected values. The coefficients of the lagged dependent variables are positively significant in the regressions as expected.

The LM test indicated no serial correlation among the residuals. The White (1980) test indicated heteroscedastic errors. Hence, all standard errors are corrected for heteroscedasticity.

5.3.2 *Estimation Results for Denmark*

The estimation results for two-digit manufacturing sectors for Denmark are reported in Table 5.3.[3] The estimation period covers the period 1982 to 1991.

The estimation results do not support the hypothesis that real exchange rate volatility has depressing effects on investment spending. Real exchange rate volatility coefficients are negatively significant only in equation (2) using total investment data and in equation (1) using investment in machinery and equipment data. The real interest rate volatility coefficients are negatively significant in the regressions without inflation rate volatility. Inflation rate volatility coefficients are statistically insignificant in the regressions.

The real exchange rate coefficients are positively significant in the regressions. This result shows that real exchange rate appreciations cause investment expansions. The real interest rate coefficients are statistically insignificant in all regressions. The inflation rate coefficients are negatively significant in the regressions using total investment data and statistically insignificant in the regressions using investment in machinery and equipment data.

The coefficients of the variable that measures openness of the economy to the international markets are positively significant in the regressions as expected in the theory. The growth rate of the real GDP coefficients are negatively significant, which is contrary to the expected values. The coefficients of the growth rate of value added are positively significant in all regressions as expected. The coefficients of lagged dependent variables are positively significant in all regressions as expected.

The LM test indicated no serial correlation among the residuals. The White (1980) test indicated heteroscedastic errors. Hence, all standard errors are corrected for heteroscedasticity.

5.3.3   Estimation Results for France

The estimation results for the French two- and three-digit manufacturing sectors are reported in Tables 5.4 and 5.5 respectively. The estimation period covers the period 1982 to 1993.

The estimation results do not show any depressing effects of real exchange rate volatility on sectoral investment. The real exchange rate volatility coefficients are statistically insignificant in all regressions.

On the other hand, real interest rate volatility has robust negatively significant effects on investment in the French manufacturing sectors. Real interest rate volatility coefficients are negatively significant in all regressions, while the real interest rate coefficients are statistically insignificant in the regressions using two-digit level sector data and negatively significant in equations (1) and (3) using three-digit level sector data. These results support the hypothesis developed by Ingersoll and Ross (1992) that real interest rate volatility has more depressing effects on investment than do the real interest rates. These results also indicate that volatility may be transferred from exchange rates to interest rates. Inflation rate volatility coefficients are negatively significant and total explanatory power (that is, adjusted R squared) increases in the regressions for the three-digit sectors.

The real exchange rate coefficients are positively significant in all regressions. This indicates that real exchange rate appreciation causes investment expansion. The inflation rate coefficients are negatively significant in the regressions together with inflation rate volatility using three-digit level sector data. They are statistically insignificant in the other regressions.

The variable that measures openness of the economy to the international markets has statistically insignificant coefficients in the regressions. The coefficients of the growth rate of the real GDP, measuring the demand variables, are positively significant in all regressions as expected. The coefficients of the growth rate of value added are negatively significant in the regressions using two-digit sector data. They are statistically insignificant in the regressions using three-digit sector data, which was unexpected.

The coefficients of the lagged dependent variables are positively significant in all regressions as expected.

The LM test indicated no serial correlation among the residuals. The White (1980) test indicated heteroscedastic errors. Hence, all standard errors are corrected for heteroscedasticity.

5.3.4 Estimation Results for Germany

The estimation results for German two-digit manufacturing sectors are reported in Table 5.6.[4] The estimation period covers the period 1982 to 1992.

The estimation results support the hypothesis that real exchange rate volatility and real interest volatility have depressing effects on investment. Real exchange rate volatility and real interest rate volatility coefficients are negatively significant in all regressions. It should be also noted that, even though Germany is a member of the ERM of the EMS, the German mark is freely floating against the non-EMS currencies and that Germany has a relatively large volume of trade with non-EMS countries. Hence, real exchange rate volatility may have negatively significant effects on investment.

The study by Artis and Taylor (1994) also found that the ERM helped to reduce volatility of the ERM member currencies against the German mark, but that the volatility of the German mark against the British pound, Japanese yen, and U.S. dollar did not change. My estimation results are consistent with this evidence. Inflation rate volatility coefficients are statistically insignificant in the regressions.

In most cases, the other coefficients have the expected signs. The real exchange rate coefficients are positively significant in all regressions, which indicates that real exchange rate appreciation has positive effects on investment spending. The real interest rate coefficients are negatively significant in the regressions together with inflation rate and inflation rate volatility. The inflation rate coefficients are negatively significant in the regressions using total investment data and statistically insignificant in the regressions using investment in machinery and equipment data.

The coefficients of the variable that measures openness of the economy to the international markets are positively significant in all regressions as expected. The coefficients of the growth rate of the real GDP are negatively significant in the regressions using total investment data and statistically insignificant in the regressions using investment in machinery and equipment data. The coefficients of the growth rate of value added are positively significant in all regressions as expected. The coefficients of the lagged dependent variables are positively significant in all equations as expected.

The LM test did not show any evidence of residual serial correlation. Since the White (1980) test indicated heteroscedastic errors, all standard errors are corrected for heteroscedasticity.

5.3.5   Estimation Results for Italy

The estimation results for two- and three-digit manufacturing sectors of Italy are reported in Tables 5.7 and 5.8 respectively. The estimation period covers the period 1981 to 1991.

The results are supportive of the hypothesis that inflation rate volatility depresses investment. Inflation rate volatility coefficients are negatively significant in the regressions, and total explanatory power (adjusted R squared) increases. Real exchange rate volatility coefficients are not statistically significant except estimate of equation (3) using two-digit level investment in on machinery and equipment and estimate of equation (2) using three-digit level investment in machinery and equipment data.

Real interest rate volatility coefficients are negatively significant in the regressions without inflation variables, possibly because both the inflation and real interest rate volatility variables act as proxies for the same source of uncertainty.

The real exchange rate coefficients are positively significant in all regressions. This is evidence that real exchange rate appreciations expand investment in the Italian manufacturing industry. The real interest rate coefficients are negatively significant only in equation (1) for three-digit sectors. The inflation rate coefficients are negatively significant in the regressions using three-digit sector data and equation (1) using two-digit level total investment data. The variable that measures the economy's openness to the international markets is dropped from the regressions due to collinearity. The coefficients of the growth rate of value added are negatively significant in the regressions using two-digit level sector data and statistically insignificant in the regressions using three-digit level sector data. The coefficients of the lagged dependent variables are positively significant in all regressions as expected.

The LM test indicated no residual serial correlation. The White (1980) test indicated heteroscedastic errors. Hence, all standard errors are corrected for heteroscedasticity.

5.3.6 Estimation Results for the Netherlands

The estimation results for two- and three-digit manufacturing sectors of the Netherlands are reported in Tables 5.9 and 5.10 respectively. The estimation period covers the period 1981 to 1992.

The estimation results do not support the hypothesis that volatility has a depressing effect on investment in the manufacturing sectors. Real exchange rate volatility coefficients are positively significant in the regressions using total investment in two-digit sectors, indicating that real exchange rate volatility causes investment expansions. Real exchange rate volatility coefficients are statistically insignificant in the other regressions.

Real interest rate volatility coefficients are statistically insignificant in all regressions. Inflation rate volatility coefficients are negatively significant in the regressions for three-digit sectors and statistically insignificant in the regressions for two-digit sectors.

The real exchange rate coefficients are negatively significant only in equations (1) and (2) using investment in machinery and equipment data at the three-digit level. This result shows that real exchange rate appreciations depress investment. The real interest rate and inflation rate coefficients are negatively significant in all regressions as expected in the theory.

The coefficient of the variable that measures the economy's openness to the international markets is statistically insignificant in all regressions, which was unexpected. The coefficients of the growth rate of the real GDP are positively significant in all regressions as expected. The coefficients of the growth rate of value added are statistically insignificant in the regressions using two-digit sector data, but are negatively significant in the regressions using three-digit sector data, which was unexpected. The coefficients of the lagged dependent variables are positively significant in all equations as expected.

The LM test did not show any evidence of residual serial correlation. Since the White (1980) test indicated heteroscedastic errors, all standard errors are corrected for heteroscedasticity.

TABLE 5.1: Estimation Results for Belgium's Two-Digit Sectors

VARIABLE NAME	COEFFICIENT					
	Total investment			Investment in machinery&equipment		
	(1)	(2)	(3)	(1)	(2)	(3)
Real exchange rate	0.9312 (1.0005)	0.5678 (0.6259)	3.3115** (1.4614)	0.5860 (1.1746)	4.6372** (2.3157)	-0.3898 (1.1305)
Real exchange rate volatility	-1.1999 (1.7939)	-1.0687 (1.7618)	-1.7091 (1.6645)	-6.8878** (3.7780)	-4.9768 (3.2990)	-0.7794 (2.9808)
Real interest rate	-0.0985 (0.0801)	-0.0745* (0.0548)	-0.1606** (0.0748)	-0.5078** (0.2051)	0.0506 (0.0732)	0.0225 (0.0437)
Real interest rate volatility	0.4173* (0.2983)	0.3324* (0.2347)	0.2851 (0.2227)	1.8166** (0.6858)	0.2455 (0.2613)	0.1106 (0.2289)
Inflation rate	-0.0599* (0.0390)	-0.0466** (0.0260)	-	-0.3038** (0.1150)	-0.0112 (0.0289)	-
Inflation rate volatility	-0.0435 (0.0896)	-	-	-0.5875** (0.2451)	-	-
Openness of the economy (-1)	0.0323 (0.7131)	-0.2076 (0.5130)	-0.2055 (0.5139)	3.3298** (1.5242)	-0.9682** (0.5258)	-0.3954 (0.4047)
Growth rate of real GDP (-1)	-0.0095 (0.0161)	-0.0079 (0.0167)	-0.0421 (0.0179)	-0.0469** (0.0266)	0.0575** (0.0336)	-0.0056 (0.0213)
Growth rate of value added (-1)	0.0003 (0.0027)	0.001 (0.0026)	-0.00006 (0.0025	-0.0013 (0.0028)	-0.0014 (0.0028)	0.0005 (0.0028)
Investment in fixed assets (-1)	0.6952** (0.0886)	0.7011** (0.0849)	0.7082** (0.0890)	-	-	-
Investment in machinery and equipment (-1)	-	-	-	0.0740** (0.0703)	0.7405** (0.0701)	0.7306** (0.0745)
Time trend	-	-	-	-	-	-
Time trend squared	-	-	-	-	-	-
Adjusted R squared	0.867	0.868	0.871	0.897	0.896	0.893
Serial correlation test (LM)	1.656	1.379	1.32	0.189	0.202	0.317

Each equation is a panel regression with 117 observations for total and 90 observations for machinery and equipment investments. (-1) shows the lag of the variable. Figures in parentheses are standard errors. Standard errors are corrected for heteroscedastic errors by using the White (1980) heteroscedasticity-robust method. The Lagrange Multiplier (LM) tests serial correlation for one lag.
* The coefficient is significant at the 10 percent level.
** The coefficient is significant at the 5 percent level.

TABLE 5.2: Estimation Results for Belgium's Three-Digit Sectors

VARIABLE NAME	COEFFICIENT					
	Total investment			Investment in machinery&equipment		
	(1)	(2)	(3)	(1)	(2)	(3)
Real exchange rate	0.0597 (0.2296)	-0.0232 (0.2265)	0.0677 (0.2707)	0.5457 (0.9845)	-0.3368 (1.0274)	0.8390 (0.9613)
Real exchange rate volatility	-0.8380 (1.5229)	-0.7477 (1.5156)	-0.9581 (1.4506)	-5.0914** (2.6760)	7.3571** (3.7217)	1.7984 (2.8562)
Real interest rate	-0.0635* (0.0391)	-0.0521* (0.0380)	-0.0350 (0.0359)	-0.4274** (0.1485)	-0.4080** (0.1402)	-0.207** (0.1214)
Real interest rate volatility	0.3009** . (0.1668)	0.3023** (0.1677)	0.0744 (0.1814)	1.500** (0.5184)	0.0597 (0.2394)	0.2181 (0.2238)
Inflation rate	-0.0491** (0.0141)	-0.0464** (0.0142)	-	-0.2628** (0.0856)	0.0929** (0.0473)	-
Inflation rate volatility	-0.0696* (0.0522)	-	-	-0.5166** (0.1943)	-	-
Openness of the economy (-1)	-0.2141 (0.3533)	-0.3355 (0.3491)	-0.6328** (0.3229)	2.9925** (1.1611)	1.2036** (0.6165)	0.4990 (0.5697)
Growth rate of real GDP (-1)	0.0259** (0.0141)	0.0297** (0.0144)	0.0135 (0.0128)	-0.003 (0.0212)	-0.1953** (0.0780)	-0.0499 (0.0523)
Growth rate of value added (-1)	-0.00004 (0.0011)	-0.0001 (0.0012)	0.00008 (0.0011)	-0.003 (0.0212)	-0.0028 (0.0023)	-0.0027 (0.0023)
Investment in fixed assets (-1)	0.5103** (0.0731)	0.5301** (0.0717)	0.5112** (0.0827)	-	-	-
Investment in machinery and equipment (-1)	-	-	-	0.585** (0.0615)	0.576** (0.0621)	0.581** (0.0633)
Time trend	-	-	18.526** (9.700)	-	237.72** (77.614)	92.27** (43.707)
Time trend squared	-	-	-0.0046** (0.0024)	-	-0.0597** (0.0184)	-0.023** (0.0109)
Adjusted R squared	0.890	0.889	0.889	0.897	0.898	0.897
Serial correlation test (LM)	1.900	1.678	1.450	0280	0.350	0.400

Each equation is a panel regression with 245 observations for total and 188 observations for machinery and equipment investments. (-1) shows the lag of the variable. Figures in parentheses are standard errors. Standard errors are corrected for heteroscedastic errors by using the White (1980) heteroscedasticity-robust method. The Lagrange Multiplier (LM) tests serial correlation for one lag.
  * The coefficient is significant at the 10 percent level.
  ** The coefficient is significant at the 5 percent level.

TABLE 5.3: Estimation Results for Denmark's Two-Digit Sectors

VARIABLE NAME	COEFFICIENT					
	Total investment			Investment in machinery&equipment		
	(1)	(2)	(3)	(1)	(2)	(3)
Real exchange rate	0.4871 (1.0902)	1.5282** (0.9039)	-1.0450 (1.7968)	0.8455 (1.6905)	2.3468** (1.3379)	3.1009** (0.6303)
Real exchange rate volatility	-1.790 (1.7638)	-2.4599* (1.7611)	3.6414 (4.2518)	-0.3688** (2.2213)	-1.2494 (2.1856)	-1.2923 (2.1773)
Real interest rate (-1)	-0.0044 (0.0148)	-0.0039 (0.0149)	0.0200 (0.0222)	0.0066 (0.0175)	0.0084 (0.0176)	0.0105 (0.0188)
Real interest rate volatility	0.0986 (0.2117)	-0.1511** (0.0672)	-0.1403** (0.0741)	0.0739 (0.2742)	-0.2698** (0.0911)	-0.287** (0.0980)
Inflation rate	-0.0522* (0.0252)	-0.0369* (0.0232)	-	-0.0482 (0.0385)	-0.0251 (0.0336)	-
Inflation rate volatility	-0.2467 (0.1944)	-	-	-0.3363 (0.2654)	-	-
Openness of the economy (-1)	3.1984** (1.0564)	4.1428** (0.9983)	3.7726** (0.9406)	5.0494** (1.5170)	6.4154** (1.4679)	6.9415** (1.2316)
Growth rate of real GDP (-1)	-0.0053 (0.0364)	-0.0436** (0.0213)	-0.0713** (0.0367)	-0.0324 (0.0432)	-0.0843** (0.0290)	-0.075** (0.0240)
Growth rate of value added (-1)	0.0106** (0.0024)	0.0111** (0.0025)	0.0103** (0.0024)	0.0093** (0.0040)	0.0099** (0.0041)	0.0095** (0.0041)
Investment in fixed assets (-1)	0.3716** (0.0887)	0.3662** (0.0891)	0.3684** (0.0867)	-	-	-
Investment in machinery and equipment (-1)	-	-	-	0.2802** (0.1489)	0.2580** (0.1479)	0.2178** (0.1221)
Time trend	-	-	65.975** (39.5474)	-	-	-
Time trend squared	-	-	-0.0165** (0.0100)	-	-	-
Adjusted R squared	0.765	0.766	0.763	0.700	0.701	0.703
Serial correlation test (LM)	0.539	0.480	0.572	2.537	2.742	2.745

Each equation is a panel regression with 90 observations. (-1) shows the lag of the variable. Figures in parentheses are standard errors. Standard errors are corrected for heteroscedastic errors by using the White (1980) heteroscedasticity-robust method. The Lagrange Multiplier (LM) tests serial correlation for one lag.
* The coefficient is significant at the 10 percent level.
** The coefficient is significant at the 5 percent level.

TABLE 5.4: Estimation Results for France's Two-Digit Sectors

VARIABLE NAME	COEFFICIENT					
	Total investment			Investment in machinery&equipment		
	(1)	(2)	(3)	(1)	(2)	(3)
Real exchange rate (-1)	1.3010** (0.5301)	1.0498** (0.3704)	1.0349** (0.3455)	1.6850** (0.6077)	1.3859** (0.4382)	1.3771** (0.4186)
Real exchange rate volatility	1.5839 (3.8223)	0.3066 (3.1037)	-0.2406 (2.2235)	-0.4217 (4.3888)	-1.8895 (3.7629)	-2.2264 (2.8260)
Real interest rate (-1)	-0.0395 (0.0388)	-0.0189 (0.0265)	-0.0135 (0.0146)	-0.0448 (0.0439)	-0.0207 (0.0308)	-0.0173 (0.0179)
Real interest rate volatility	-0.1940** (0.0592)	-0.1805** (0.0567)	-0.1807** (0.0569)	-0.2418** (0.0687)	-0.2255** (0.0661)	-0.2256** (0.0662)
Inflation rate	-0.0077 (0.0140)	-0.0027 (0.0120)	-	-0.0076 (0.0156)	-0.0016 (0.0134)	-
Inflation rate volatility	-0.0310 (0.0418)	-	-	-0.0366 (0.0473)	-	-
Openness of the economy (-1)	-0.0310 (0.0418)	-0.2262 (0.2230)	-0.1987 (0.2016)	-0.2378 (0.2860)	-0.2750 (0.2859)	-0.2581 (0.2602)
Growth rate of real GDP (-1)	0.0541** (0.0096)	0.0551** (0.0092)	0.0545** (0.0092)	0.4495** (0.0832)	0.0554** (0.0107)	0.0550** (0.0104)
Growth rate of value added (-1)	-0.0018** (0.0008)	-0.002** (0.0008)	-0.002** (0.0007)	-0.0019** (0.0008)	-0.0021** (0.0009)	-0.0021** (0.0009)
Investment in fixed assets (-1)	0.4290** (0.0838)	0.4429** (0.0842)	0.4420** (0.0846)	-	-	-
Investment in machinery and equipment (-1)	-	-	-	0.4495** (0.0832)	0.4660** (0.0831)	0.4657** (0.0832)
Time trend	-	-	-	-	-	-
Time trend squared	-	-	-	-	-	-
Adjusted R squared	0.873	0.874	0.875	0.846	0.847	0.848
Serial correlation test (LM)	1.743	1.264	1.199	1.740	1.014	0.980

Each equation is a panel regression with 96 observations. (-1) shows the lag of the variable. Figures in parentheses are standard errors. Standard errors are corrected for heteroscedastic errors by using the White (1980) heteroscedasticity-robust method. The Lagrange Multiplier (LM) tests serial correlation for one lag.
* The coefficient is significant at the 10 percent level.
** The coefficient is significant at the 5 percent level.

TABLE 5.5: Estimation Results for France's Three-Digit Sectors

VARIABLE NAME	COEFFICIENT					
	Total investment			Investment in machinery&equipment		
	(1)	(2)	(3)	(1)	(2)	(3)
Real exchange rate (-1)	1.2447** (0.5817)	0.5146* (0.3790)	0.4857* (0.3735)	1.5804** (0.6623)	0.6209* (0.4454)	0.5993* (0.4413)
Real exchange rate volatility	4.5675 (4.4092)	0.7826 (3.6819)	-0.3464 (2.5537)	4.2915 (4.8837)	-0.6665 (4.1058)	-1.5277 (2.8824)
Real interest rate (-1)	-0.0883** (0.0388)	-0.0306 (0.0239)	-0.0194* (0.0136)	-0.1067** (0.0444)	-0.0309 (0.0276)	-0.0224* (0.0167)
Real interest rate volatility	-0.1990** (0.0494)	-0.1647** (0.0471)	-0.1650** (0.0471)	-0.2714** (0.0591)	-0.2263** (0.0563)	-0.2266** (0.0564)
Inflation rate	-0.020* (0.0142)	-0.0056 (0.0110)	-	-0.0232* (0.0161)	-0.0043 (0.0125)	-
Inflation rate volatility	-0.0858** (0.0439)	-	-	-0.1128** (0.0487)	-	-
Openness of the economy (-1)	0.0412 (0.2416)	-0.0283 (0.2420)	0.0283 (0.2077)	0.1017 (0.2784)	0.0069 (0.2798)	0.0501 (0.2439)
Growth rate of real GDP (-1)	0.0404** (0.0089)	0.0444** (0.0087)	0.0430** (0.0082)	0.0409** (0.0105)	0.0460** (0.0106)	0.0501** (0.2439)
Growth rate of value added (-1)	-0.0002 (0.0009)	-0.0006 (0.0009)	-0.0006 (0.0009)	0.0001 (0.001)	-0.0003 (0.0011)	-0.0003** (0.0011)
Investment in fixed assets (-1)	0.4641** (0.0592)	0.4737** (0.0591)	0.4733** (0.0593)	-	-	-
Investment in machinery and equipment (-1)	-	-	-	0.4378** (0.0556)	0.4512** (0.0565)	0.4512** (0.0565)
Time trend	-	-	-	-	-	-
Time trend squared	-	-	-	-	-	-
Adjusted R squared	0.897	0.895	0.895	0.880	0.876	0.877
Serial correlation test (LM)	0.629	0.0716	0.0419	1.969	0.471	0.404

Each equation is a panel regression with 204 observations. (-1) shows the lag of the variable. Figures in parentheses are standard errors. Standard errors are corrected for heteroscedastic errors by using the White (1980) heteroscedasticity-robust method. The Lagrange Multiplier (LM) tests serial correlation for one lag.
* The coefficient is significant at the 10 percent level.
** The coefficient is significant at the 5 percent level.

TABLE 5.6: Estimation Results for Germany's Two-Digit Sectors

VARIABLE NAME	COEFFICIENT					
	Total investment			Investment in machinery&equipment		
	(1)	(2)	(3)	(1)	(2)	(3)
Real exchange rate	1.1667** (0.2387)	1.1966** (0.2421)	1.3968** (0.2624)	1.2621** (0.2613)	1.2362** (0.2662)	1.3517** (0.2772)
Real exchange rate volatility	-4.1249** (1.1643)	-4.085** (1.1653)	-2.9266** (1.0711)	-3.2372** (1.1845)	-3.2821** (1.1827)	-0.2661** (0.9695)
Real interest rate (-1)	-0.0363** (0.0145)	-0.037** (0.0147)	-0.0113 (0.0142)	-0.0295** (0.0139)	-0.0289** (0.0142)	-0.0150 (0.0128)
Real interest rate volatility	-0.0363** (0.0636)	-0.2084** (0.0562)	-0.2724** (0.0593)	-0.216** (0.0664)	-0.2028** (0.0591)	-0.2376** (0.0543)
Inflation rate	-0.0241** (0.0078)	-0.0242** (0.0078)	-	-0.0132 (0.0114)	-0.0131 (0.0115)	-
Inflation rate volatility	0.0212 (0.0347)	-	-	-0.0236 (0.0369)	-	-
Openness of the economy (-1)	2.4755** (0.726)	2.6045** (0.7099)	3.201** (0.7506)	2.7411** (0.7561)	2.5952** (0.7548)	2.9252** (0.7956)
Growth rate of real GDP (-1)	-0.0175** (0.0123)	-0.0204** (0.0105)	-0.03** (0.0111)	-0.0134 (0.0134)	-0.0101 (0.0116)	-0.0158* (0.0116)
Growth rate of value added (-1)	0.0076** (0.0024)	0.0076** (0.0024)	0.0069** (0.0025)	0.0044* (0.0028)	0.0044* (0.0028)	-0.004* (0.0028)
Investment in fixed assets (-1)	0.448** (0.0892)	0.4493** (0.0894)	0.4238** (0.0932)	-	-	-
Investment in machinery and equipment (-1)	-	-	-	0.3626** (0.1231)	0.3557** (0.1193)	0.3387** (0.1284)
Time trend	-	-	-	-	-	-
Time trend squared	-	-	-	-	-	-
Adjusted R squared	0.912	0.913	0.903	0.894	0.896	0.895
Serial correlation test (LM)	0.485	0.562	0.130	0.078	0.112	0.455

Each equation is a panel regression with 77 observations. (-1) shows the lag of the variable. Figures in parentheses are standard errors. Standard errors are corrected for heteroscedastic errors by using the White (1980) heteroscedasticity-robust method. The Lagrange Multiplier (LM) tests serial correlation for one lag.
  * The coefficient is significant at the 10 percent level.
  ** The coefficient is significant at the 5 percent level.

TABLE 5.7: Estimation Results for Italy's Two-Digit Sectors

VARIABLE NAME	COEFFICIENT					
	Total investment			Investment in machinery&equipment		
	(1)	(2)	(3)	(1)	(2)	(3)
Real exchange rate	1.0539** (0.6047)	1.1206** (0.6036)	1.2478** (0.6041)	1.1225** (0.6503)	1.2914** (0.6604)	1.2331** (0.6484)
Real exchange rate volatility	2.5237 (2.9028)	2.9885 (2.8006)	1.1221 (2.479)	2.2648 (3.009)	2.9118 (2.9599)	3.6278* (2.5796)
Real interest rate	-0.0329 (0.0407)	0.00001 (0.0333)	0.0213 (0.0272)	-0.0233 (0.0434)	0.0371 (0.0335)	0.0292 (0.0275)
Real interest rate volatility	0.0540 (0.0542)	0.0174 (0.0553)	-0.0509** (0.0191)	-0.008 (0.0584)	-0.077* (0.0585)	-0.0521** (0.0204)
Inflation rate	-0.0344** (0.017)	-0.0205 (0.0166)	-	-0.018 (0.0185)	0.0077 (0.0177)	-
Inflation rate volatility	-0.0495* (0.0328)	-	-	-0.0884** (0.0329)	-	-
Openness of the economy (-1)	-	-	-	-	-	-
Growth rate of real GDP (-1)	-0.0335 (0.0319)	0.00023 (0.0255)	0.0276** (0.0122)	-0.02** (0.0342)	0.0429** (0.0238)	0.0326** (0.0108)
Growth rate of value added (-1)	-0.0018** (0.0008)	-0.0017** (0.0008)	-0.0019** (0.0007)	-0.0025* (0.0007)	-0.0024* (0.0007)	-0.0023** (0.0007)
Investment in fixed assets (-1)	0.1829** (0.1107)	0.195** (0.1117)	0.1633** (0.1082)	-	-	-
Investment in machinery and equipment (-1)	-	-	-	0.1033** (0.0981)	0.0989** (0.1024)	0.1123** (0.1022)
Time trend	-	-	-	-	-	-
Time trend squared	-	-	-	-	-	-
Adjusted R squared	0.840	0.838	0.838	0.845	0.829	0.831
Serial correlation test (LM)	0.346	0.249	0.530	0.090	0.0836	0.110

Each equation is a panel regression with 99 observations. (-1) shows the lag of the variable. Figures in parentheses are standard errors. Standard errors are corrected for heteroscedastic errors by using the White (1980) heteroscedasticity-robust method. The Lagrange Multiplier (LM) tests serial correlation for one lag.
* The coefficient is significant at the 10 percent level.
** The coefficient is significant at the 5 percent level.

TABLE 5.8: Estimation Results for Italy's Two-Digit Sectors

VARIABLE NAME	COEFFICIENT					
	Total investment			Investment in machinery&equipment		
	(1)	(2)	(3)	(1)	(2)	(3)
Real exchange rate	1.0911** (0.6337)	1.2338** (0.6319)	1.3887** (0.6346)	1.371** (0.7056)	1.5653** (0.7045)	1.6398** (0.7101)
Real exchange rate volatility	2.8526 (3.3886)	3.4556 (3.38)	0.5923 (2.9648)	4.0165 (3.5947)	4.6816* (3.5369)	3.6126 (3.2387)
Real interest rate	-0.0886** (0.0394)	-0.037 (0.0315)	-0.0053 (0.0275)	-0.0671* (0.0477)	-0.003 (0.0358)	0.0083 (0.0297)
Real interest rate volatility	0.1006* (0.0665)	0.0419 (0.0593)	-0.0622** (0.0174)	0.0584 (0.0735)	-0.0155 (0.0642)	-0.0533 (0.0186)
Inflation rate	-0.0533** (0.0193)	-0.0315** (0.0162)	-	-0.0389** (0.0222)	-0.0114 (0.0183)	-
Inflation rate volatility	-0.0754** (0.0296)	-	-	-0.093** (0.0348)	-	-
Openness of the economy (-1)	-	-	-	-	-	-
Growth rate of real GDP (-1)	-0.0907** (0.0354)	-0.037* (0.0249)	0.0035 (0.0116)	-0.0708** (0.0424)	-0.0037 (0.0283)	0.0109 (0.0131)
Growth rate of value added (-1)	0.0001 (0.001)	0.00029 (0.001)	-0.00002 (0.001)	-0.0003 (0.001)	-0.0002 (0.001)	-0.0003 (0.001)
Investment in fixed assets (-1)	0.3332** (0.0903)	0.3316** (0.0904)	0.3015** (0.0841)	-	-	-
Investment in machinery and equipment (-1)	-	-	-	0.2265** (0.0876)	0.219** (0.0867)	0.2049** (0.0831)
Time trend	-	-	-	-	-	-
Time trend squared	-	-	-	-	-	-
Adjusted R squared	0.822	0.819	0.817	0.818	0.814	0.814
Serial correlation test (LM)	1.031	1.755	2.516	0.104	1.183	1.642

Each equation is a panel regression with 264 observations. (-1) shows the lag of the variable. Figures in parentheses are standard errors. Standard errors are corrected for heteroscedastic errors by using the White (1980) heteroscedasticity-robust method. The Lagrange Multiplier (LM) tests serial correlation for one lag.
* The coefficient is significant at the 10 percent level.
** The coefficient is significant at the 5 percent level.

TABLE 5.9: Estimation Results for the Netherlands' Two-Digit Sectors

VARIABLE NAME	COEFFICIENT					
	Total investment			Investment in machinery&equipment		
	(1)	(2)	(3)	(1)	(2)	(3)
Real exchange rate	-0.7058 (1.283)	-0.8081 (0.9881)	-0.1903 (0.9256)	-0.3391 (1.3611)	-0.6077 (1.0799)	-0.1173 (1.0369)
Real exchange rate volatility	3.5317* (2.7111)	3.9859** (2.0849)	4.3124** (1.9486)	1.3708 (3.2125)	2.5794 (2.4053)	1.7732 (2.7609)
Real interest rate (-2)	-0.0839** (0.0324)	-0.0876** (0.0293)	-0.0711** (0.0331)	-0.0531* (0.0342)	-0.0628** (0.0302)	-0.0406* (0.0316)
Real interest rate volatility	-0.0102 (0.1188)	-0.0406 (0.1421)	-0.0308 (0.1417)	0.2635 (0.1828)	0.1826 (0.1893)	-0.2146 (0.1841)
Inflation rate	-0.0286** (0.0105)	-0.0276** (0.0093)	-	-0.0188* (0.0135)	-0.0161* (0.0121)	-
Inflation rate volatility	-0.028 (0.133)	-	-	-0.0745 (0.1448)	-	-
Openness of the economy (-1)	-0.1253 (0.2858)	-0.1796 (0.1889)	-0.1484 (0.1793)	0.1142 (0.319)	-0.0303 (0.2138)	0.0524 (0.1985)
Growth rate of real GDP (-1)	0.0659** (0.0219)	0.0663** (0.0229)	0.0659** (0.0255)	0.0878** (0.0268)	0.0889** (0.0278)	0.1002** (0.024)
Growth rate of value added (-1)	-0.0003 (0.0004)	-0.0003 (0.0003)	-0.0003 (0.0004)	0.0003 (0.0005)	-0.0003 (0.0005)	0.0002 (0.0004)
Investment in fixed assets (-1)	0.5579** (0.1511)	0.5589** (0.149)	0.5564** (0.149)	-	-	-
Investment in machinery and equipment (-1)	-	-	-	0.5053** (0.1549)	0.5073** (0.1528)	0.5025** (0.1518)
Time trend	-	-	18.62** (6.8901)	-	-	-
Time trend squared	-	-	-0.0046** (0.0017)	-	-	-
Adjusted R squared	0.708	0.711	0.707	0.716	0.718	0.718
Serial correlation test (LM)	0.472	0.469	0.426	1.936	1.928	1.06

Each equation is a panel regression with 108 observations. (-1) shows the lag of the variable. Figures in parentheses are standard errors. Standard errors are corrected for heteroscedastic errors by using the White (1980) heteroscedasticity-robust method. The Lagrange Multiplier (LM) tests serial correlation for one lag.
  * The coefficient is significant at the 10 percent level.
  ** The coefficient is significant at the 5 percent level.

TABLE 5.10: Estimation Results for the Netherlands' Three-Digit Sectors

VARIABLE NAME	COEFFICIENT					
	Total investment			Investment in machinery&equipment		
	(1)	(2)	(3)	(1)	(2)	(3)
Real exchange rate	-0.3872 (0.6789)	-0.5406 (0.6898)	-0.1827 (0.7006)	-0.9945* (0.6824)	-1.125* (0.6921)	-0.7782 (0.7089)
Real exchange rate volatility	-0.0015 (1.5088)	1.5564 (1.3993)	1.8344* (1.3433)	-0.2902 (1.5755)	0.9926 (1.4188)	1.0808 (1.3552)
Real interest rate (-2)	-0.0287* (0.0193)	-0.026* (0.0193)	-0.0199 (0.0215)	-0.0331** (0.0194)	-0.031* (0.0196)	-0.0233 (0.022)
Real interest rate volatility	0.0706 (0.1435)	-0.0297 (0.1237)	-0.0051 (0.1175)	0.1442 (0.1466)	0.0615 (0.1268)	0.0876 (0.1211)
Inflation rate	-0.0358** (0.0104)	-0.0302** (0.0103)	-	-0.0355** (0.0105)	-0.0309** (0.0104)	-
Inflation rate volatility	-0.1242** (0.0724)	-	-	-0.1024* (0.0747)	-	-
Openness of the economy (-1)	0.0759 (0.1693)	-0.0495 (0.1492)	-0.1073 (0.2031)	0.1652 (0.1659)	0.0628 (0.1445)	-0.011 (0.2004)
Growth rate of real GDP (-1)	0.4257** (0.0183)	0.0474** (0.0184)	0.0431** (0.0202)	0.0411** (0.0187)	0.0448** (0.0188)	0.0424** (0.0205)
Growth rate of value added (-1)	-0.0012** (0.0005)	-0.0011** (0.0005)	-0.0011** (0.0005)	-0.0012** (0.0006)	-0.0011** (0.0006)	-0.001** (0.0006)
Investment in fixed assets (-1)	0.4257** (0.0902)	0.4234** (0.09)	0.4298** (0.0892)	-	-	-
Investment in machinery and equipment (-1)	-	-	-	0.4688** (0.0901)	0.4685** (0.09009)	0.4732** (0.0903)
Time trend	-	-	24.543** (8.0411)	-	-	23.39** (8.2532)
Time trend squared	-	-	-0.0061** (0.002)	-	-	-0.0058** (0.002)
Adjusted R squared	0.76	0.759	0.759	0.794	0.794	0.794
Serial correlation test (LM)	1.053	1.207	1.286	1.86	1.54	1.39

Each equation is a panel regression with 275 observations. (-1) shows the lag of the variable. Figures in parentheses are standard errors. Standard errors are corrected for heteroscedastic errors by using the White (1980) heteroscedasticity-robust method. The Lagrange Multiplier (LM) tests serial correlation for one lag.
 * The coefficient is significant at the 10 percent level.
 ** The coefficient is significant at the 5 percent level.

5.4 Estimation Results for the Countries in the Flexible Exchange Rate System

In this section, the estimation results for the countries in the flexible exchange rate system are presented. The estimation results support the hypothesis that real exchange rate volatility has depressing effects on sectoral investment in the flexible exchange rate system.

Real interest rate volatility has depressing effects on investment in the United Kingdom, although the significance of the coefficients in the other countries varies from regression to regression. Real interest rate volatility has positively significant effects on investment in the United States and Norway. Inflation rate volatility has depressing effects on investment in Norway.

5.4.1 Estimation Results for Finland

The estimation results for Finland's two- and three-digit manufacturing sectors are reported in Tables 5.11 and 5.12 respectively. The estimation period covers the period 1982 to 1991.

The estimation results support the hypothesis that real exchange rate volatility has depressing effects on investment spending. Real exchange rate volatility coefficients are negatively significant in the regressions using three-digit level data and equations (2) and (3) using two-digit level total investment data.

Real interest rate volatility has mixed effects on sectoral investment. Real interest rate volatility coefficients are positively significant in the regressions using two-digit level data. However, they are negatively significant in the regressions together with inflation variables using three-digit level data, showing that there is an inverse collinearity between these variables. Inflation rate volatility coefficients is positively significant in the regression using three-digit level total investment data. They are statistically insignificant in the other regressions.

The real exchange rate coefficients are negatively significant in the regressions. This result shows that real exchange appreciation causes investment contraction. The real interest rate coefficients are negatively significant only in equations (1) and (2) using total investment data at the three-digit level. The inflation rate coefficients are negatively significant in the regressions using two-digit level data, and positively significant in the regressions using three-digit level data.

The variable that measures openness of the economy to the international markets is dropped from the regressions due to collinearity. The growth rate of the real GDP is also dropped from the regressions due to collinearity with the growth rate of value added. The growth rate of value added coefficients are negatively significant in the regressions using two-digit level total investment data and statistically insignificant in the other regressions. The lagged dependent variables coefficients are positively significant in all regressions as expected.

The LM test indicated no serial correlation among the residuals. The White (1980) test indicated heteroscedastic errors. Hence, all standard errors are corrected for heteroscedasticity.

5.4.2 Estimation Results for Norway

The estimation results for Norwegian two- and three-digit manufacturing sectors are reported in Tables 5.13 and 5.14 respectively. The estimation period covers the period 1980 to 1991.

The estimation results are supportive of the hypothesis that real exchange rate volatility depresses investment. Real exchange rate volatility coefficients are negatively significant. Real interest rate volatility coefficients are positively significant in the regressions without inflation rate and inflation rate volatility. Inflation rate volatility coefficients are negatively significant in all regressions and total explanatory power (adjusted R squared) increases. This result provides that inflation rate volatility has depressing effects on investment.

The real exchange rate coefficients are negatively significant in the regressions. This result shows that real exchange rate appreciations have depressing effects on sectoral investment. The real interest rate coefficients are positively significant in all regressions. This result is consistent with the theory developed by Ingersoll and Ross (1992). An increase in the real interest rates increases investment in the short run by increasing the cost of waiting. The inflation rate coefficients are also positively significant in the regressions. This result indicates that inflation may stimulate investment. Odeh (1968) and Pindyck and Solimano (1993) also showed that moderate inflation may induce investment spending.

The variable that measures openness of the economy to the international markets is dropped from the regressions due to collinearity. The growth rate of the real GDP is dropped from the regressions due to collinearity with the growth rate of value added. The coefficients of the growth rate of value added are statistically insignificant or negatively significant, which was not expected. The coefficients of the lagged dependent variables are positively significant in the regressions as expected.

The LM test indicated no serial correlation among the residuals. The White (1980) test indicated heteroscedastic errors. Hence, all standard errors are corrected for heteroscedasticity.

5.4.3 Estimation Results for the United Kingdom

The estimation results for the United Kingdom's two- and three-digit manufacturing sectors are reported in Tables 5.15 and 5.16 respectively. The estimation period covers the period 1979 to 1992.

The estimation results support the theory that real exchange rate volatility has depressing effects on sectoral investment. Real exchange rate volatility coefficients are negatively significant in all regressions. Real interest rate volatility coefficients are also negatively significant in the regressions, while the real interest rate coefficients are statistically insignificant. This result is also consistent with the theory developed by Ingersoll and Ross (1992). Real interest rate volatility can have more depressing effects on investment than do the real interest rate levels. Inflation rate volatility coefficients are negatively significant in the regressions using total investment data.

The real exchange rate coefficients are positively significant in the regressions, which shows that real exchange rate appreciation cause investment expansion. The inflation rate coefficients are negatively significant only in equation (2) using investment in machinery and equipment data.

The variable that measures the economy's openness to the international markets has a positive sign and is statistically significant in the regressions as expected. This result provides that openness to the international markets increases investment through specialization. The coefficients of the growth rate of the real GDP are positively significant in all regressions as expected. The coefficients of the growth rate of value added are positively significant in all regressions as expected. An increase in net output spurs investment. The coefficients of the lagged dependent variables are positive and statistically significant as expected.

The LM test indicated no residual serial correlation except for the regressions using the three-digit level total investment data. The White (1980) test indicated heteroscedastic errors. Hence, all standard errors are corrected for heteroscedasticity.

5.4.4 Estimation Results for the United States

The estimation results for the United States' two- and three-digit manufacturing sectors are reported in Tables 5.17 and 5.18 respectively. The estimation period covers the period 1980 to 1992.

The estimation results are not generally supportive of the hypothesis that volatility depresses investment expenditures. Real exchange rate volatility and inflation rate volatility coefficients are statistically significant only in the regressions using total investment data in the U.S. three-digit manufacturing sectors.

Campa and Goldberg (1995) and Goldberg (1993) also found that real exchange rate volatility has no depressing effects on investment in U.S. industry.

Real interest rate volatility coefficients are positively significant in the regressions, implying that real interest rate volatility stimulates investment. This result contradicts the hypothesis that real interest rate volatility depresses investment.

The real exchange rate coefficients are positively significant in the regressions, indicating that real exchange rate appreciations stimulate investment spending. This result is very likely because most U.S. manufacturing sectors became net importers in the 1980s (Campa and Goldberg, 1995; Goldberg, 1993). Therefore, an increase in the real exchange rate increases investment spending.

The real interest rate coefficients are negatively significant in the regressions, showing that increases in real interest rate depress investment. The inflation rate coefficients are negatively significant in the regressions and total explanatory power (adjusted R squared) increases.

The variable that measures the economy's openness to the international markets has a positive sign and is statistically significant in the regressions as expected. The growth rate of the real GDP is dropped from the regressions due to collinearity with the growth rate of value added. The coefficients of the growth rate of value added are positively significant as expected; an increase in net output stimulates investment spending. The coefficients of the lagged dependent variables are positively significant in the regressions as expected.

The LM test indicated no residual serial correlation. The White (1980) test indicated heteroscedastic errors. Hence, all standard errors are corrected for heteroscedasticity.

5.5 Conclusion

In this section, estimation results of the three investment equations are presented for the EMS countries, as well as for the countries in the flexible exchange rate system. The estimation results support the hypothesis that real exchange rate volatility has depressing effects on sectoral investment in the flexible exchange rate system. The only exception was the United States, which has a relatively closed economy.

In the EMS countries, real exchange rate volatility has depressing effects on investment only in Germany, which has a large trade volume with non-EMS countries. Real interest rate volatility has depressing effects on investment in Denmark, France, Germany, and the United Kingdom. Inflation rate volatility has depressing effects on investment in France, Italy, and Norway. The inflation rate has depressing effects on investment in Belgium, Germany, the Netherlands, Norway, and the United States.

The previous study by Pindyck and Solimano (1993) did not show the statistically significant effects of real exchange rate volatility, because they used aggregate investment data, rather than sector-specific data. Goldberg (1993) used sector-specific data for the United States, which has a relatively closed economy.

This study used sector-specific data for these open economies. The empirical results show more clearly the effects of changes in the real exchange rate levels and volatility on investment in the sectors that may be predominantly export-oriented, import-oriented, or closed to international trade. A more ideal test would be to use interactive variables to measure export- and import-orientation and "openness" to international trade of each sector to accurately capture the effects of real exchange rates and volatility on real investment behavior.

Therefore, the second step of this study will be the re-estimation of equations (1) through (3) using interactive variables. Sector-specific foreign trade data are available for Finland, Norway, the United Kingdom, and the United States. The re-estimation results are reported in Chapter 6.

NOTES

1. The sample size changes from country to country depending on the availability of investment data, These sample changes are noted during the reporting of estimation results.

2. Detailed information about testing serial correlation in the presence of lagged dependent variable in the regressions is contained in Greene (1993), p. 428; Maddala (1992), pp. 248-250; and White (1980).

3. Investment data for the three-digit manufacturing sectors is not available. For that reason, only investment in the two-digit manufacturing sectors is used in the estimation.

4. Investment data for the three-digit manufacturing sectors is not available. For that reason, only investment in the two-digit manufacturing sectors is used in the estimation.

TABLE 5.11: Estimation Results for Finland's Two-Digit Sectors

VARIABLE NAME	COEFFICIENT					
	Total investment			Investment in machinery&equipment		
	(1)	(2)	(3)	(1)	(2)	(3)
Real exchange rate	-0.1163** (0.0581)	-0.1162** (0.0582)	-0.1318** (0.0634)	-0.0524 (0.0477)	-0.0534 (0.0480)	-0.0642** (0.0550)
Real exchange rate volatility	0.7449 (1.2275)	1.4116** (0.6296)	0.0687** (0.1011)	-0.8476 (1.1805)	0.0807 (0.0937)	0.4201 (0.5837)
Real interest rate	0.0596 (0.0596)	0.1069 (0.1007)	0.0687 (0.1011)	0.0098 (0.1347)	0.0274 (0.0077)	0.0470 (0.0940)
Real interest rate volatility	0.0328* (0.0225)	0.0211** (0.0081)	0.0232** (0.0081)	0.0455** (0.0205)	0.0274** (0.0077)	0.0293 (0.0075)
Inflation rate	-4.6719** (1.9768)	-0.7951** (1.9679)	-	-3.9941** (1.8185)	-4.1704** (1.8380)	-
Inflation rate volatility	0.02109 (0.0402)	-	-	0.0323 (0.0377)	-	-
Openness of the economy (-1)	-	-	-	-	-	-
Growth rate of real GDP (-1)	-	-	-	-	-	-
Growth rate of value added (-1)	-0.0072** (0.0029)	-0.007** (0.0029)	-0.0065** (0.003)	-0.0031 (0.0028)	-0.0033 (0.0029)	-0.0024 (0.003)
Investment in fixed assets (-1)	0.2315** (0.1033)	0.2412** (0.1040)	0.1915** (0.1086)	-	-	-
Investment in machinery and equipment (-1)	-	-	-	0.3030** (0.1169)	0.3223** (0.1180)	0.2921** (0.1207)
Time trend	-	-	-	-	-	-
Time trend squared	-	-	-	-	-	-
Adjusted R squared	0.699	0.703	0.685	0.751	0.752	0.740
Serial correlation test (LM)	2.357	1.990	2.173	1.027	0.719	1.030

Each equation is a panel regression with 90 observations. (-1) shows the lag of the variable. Figures in parentheses are standard errors. Standard errors are corrected for heteroscedastic errors by using the White (1980) heteroscedasticity-robust method. The Lagrange Multiplier (LM) tests serial correlation for one lag.
* The coefficient is significant at the 10 percent level.
** The coefficient is significant at the 5 percent level.

TABLE 5.12: Estimation Results for Finland's Three-Digit Sectors

VARIABLE NAME	COEFFICIENT					
	Total investment			Investment in machinery&equipment		
	(1)	(2)	(3)	(1)	(2)	(3)
Real exchange rate	-0.6198** (0.1108)	-0.5673** (0.1062)	-0.4183** (0.0614)	-0.5266** (0.0993)	-0.5273** (0.100)	-0.4316** (0.0704)
Real exchange rate volatility	-2.7980 (1.5681)	-2.7018** (1.5907)	-2.7763** (1.6057)	-1.847** (1.3803)	-1.8476* (1.3784)	-2.1387 (1.3337)
Real interest rate	0.0678** (0.0361)	0.0495* (0.0339)	-0.0089 (0.0144)	0.0288 (0.0280)	0.0290 (0.0271)	-0.0090 (0.0159)
Real interest rate volatility	-0.3097** (0.1185)	-0.2168** (0.1073)	-0.0761 (0.0768)	-0.2995** (0.1073)	-0.3015 (0.1168)	-0.1945 (0.0887)
Inflation rate	0.0936** (0.0452)	0.0841** (0.0451)	-	0.0571* (0.0364)	0.0569 (0.0361)	-
Inflation rate volatility	0.1904** (0.0898)	-	-	-0.0051 (0.0929)	-	-
Openness of the economy (-1)	-	-	-	-	-	-
Growth rate of real GDP (-1)	-	-	-	-	-	-
Growth rate of value added (-1)	0.0015 (0.0029)	0.0016 (0.0029)	0.0013 (0.0029)	0.0024 (0.0026)	0.0024 (0.0026)	0.0021 (0.0026)
Investment in fixed assets (-1)	0.2055** (0.0912)	0.2025** (0.0941)	0.2198** (0.0941)	-	-	-
Investment in machinery and equipment (-1)	-	-	-	0.2475** (0.1046)	0.2475** (0.1043)	0.2567** (0.1074)
Time trend	-	-	-	-	-	-
Time trend squared	-	-	-	-	-	-
Adjusted R squared	0.368	0.364	0.362	0.431	0.433	0.432
Serial correlation test (LM)	2.480	1.860	2.250	1.285	0.920	1.200

Each equation is a panel regression with 332 observations. (-1) shows the lag of the variable. Figures in parentheses are standard errors. Standard errors are corrected for heteroscedastic errors by using the White (1980) heteroscedasticity-robust method. The Lagrange Multiplier (LM) tests serial correlation for one lag.
* The coefficient is significant at the 10 percent level.
** The coefficient is significant at the 5 percent level.

TABLE 5.13: Estimation Results for Norway's Two-Digit Sectors

VARIABLE NAME	COEFFICIENT					
	Total investment			Investment in machinery&equipment		
	(1)	(2)	(3)	(1)	(2)	(3)
Real exchange rate	-2.1226** (1.1386)	-1.1955 (1.0884)	-1.1840 (1.0856)	-2.9257** (1.2117)	-2.1227** (1.2424)	-2.1141** (1.2420)
Real exchange rate volatility	-6.0054** (3.3233)	-7.7817** (3.3393)	-6.0700** (3.5639)	-4.8237* (3.2852)	-6.7528** (3.2214)	-5.0695* (3.3845)
Real interest rate (-1)	0.0926** (0.0196)	0.0817** (0.02008)	0.0845** (0.0205)	0.0748** (0.0176)	0.0647** (0.0176)	0.0675** (0.0182)
Real interest rate volatility	0.1152 (0.1980)	0.0715 (0.2042)	0.3719** (0.080)	0.0318 (0.2016)	-0.0062 (0.2050)	0.290** (0.0727)
Inflation rate	0.0841** (0.0384)	0.0682** (0.0382)	-	0.0837** (0.0394)	0.0673** (0.0407)	-
Inflation rate volatility	-0.1150** (0.0486)	-	-	-0.1087** (0.0565)	-	-
Openness of the economy (-1)	-	-	-	-	-	-
Growth rate of real GDP (-1)	-	-	-	-	-	-
Growth rate of value added (-1)	-0.0006 (0.0016)	-0.0014 (0.0017)	-0.0008 (0.0016)	-0.0024* (0.0017)	-0.0030** (0.0017)	-0.0024* (0.0016)
Investment in fixed assets (-1)	0.4349** (0.0944)	0.4244** (0.0939)	0.4473** (0.0889)	-	-	-
Investment in machinery and equipment (-1)	-	-	-	0.2822** (0.1012)	0.2924** (0.0985)	0.3180** (0.0934)
Time trend	-	-	-	-	-	-
Time trend squared	-	-	-	-	-	-
Adjusted R squared	0.725	0.713	0.708	0.678	0.667	0.662
Serial correlation test (LM)	0.080	0.085	0.174	0.293	0.868	1.029

Each equation is a panel regression with 108 observations. (-1) shows the lag of the variable. Figures in parentheses are standard errors. Standard errors are corrected for heteroscedastic errors by using the White (1980) heteroscedasticity-robust method. The Lagrange Multiplier (LM) tests serial correlation for one lag.
   * The coefficient is significant at the 10 percent level.
   ** The coefficient is significant at the 5 percent level.

TABLE 5.14: Estimation Results for Norway's Three-Digit Sectors

VARIABLE NAME	COEFFICIENT					
	Total investment			Investment in machinery&equipment		
	(1)	(2)	(3)	(1)	(2)	(3)
Real exchange rate	-0.5029 (1.1693)	-2.1425* (1.6158)	-2.2575* (1.6043)	-2.1937** (1.0883)	-4.0031** (1.5861)	-4.1388** (1.5758)
Real exchange rate volatility	-3.8894 (4.2447)	-8.4752* (5.5608)	0.8293 (4.5109)	-4.2248* (4.021)	-14.628** (5.0768)	-3.3441 (4.3322)
Real interest rate (-1)	0.0761** (0.0143)	0.0537** (0.0149)	0.0520** (0.0149)	0.0758** (0.0130)	0.0513** (0.0145)	0.0491** (0.0148)
Real interest rate volatility	-0.0239 (0.1494)	-0.0400 (0.1734)	0.3632** (0.077)	-0.0011 (0.1433)	-0.1258 (0.1593)	0.3637** (0.0734)
Inflation rate	0.1232** (0.0334)	0.1216** (0.0499)	-	0.1098** (0.031)	0.1477** (0.043)	-
Inflation rate volatility	-0.1059** (0.0459)	-	-	-0.1350** (0.0463)	-	-
Openness of the economy (-1)	-	-	-	-	-	-
Growth rate of real GDP (-1)	-	-	-	-	-	-
Growth rate of value added (-1)	-0.0012 (0.0017)	-0.0012 (0.0017)	-0.0010 (0.0017)	-0.0022* (0.0016)	-0.0022* (0.0016)	-0.0020 (0.0015)
Investment in fixed assets (-1)	0.2332** (0.1292)	0.2247** (0.1299)	0.2347** (0.1295)	-	-	-
Investment in machinery and equipment (-1)	-	-	-	0.1621** (0.0982)	0.1579* (0.0981)	0.1696** (0.0992)
Time trend	-	23.253** (13.343)	35.649** (12.030)	-	19.534** (13.115)	34.627** (12.306)
Time trend squared	-	-0.005** (0.003)	-0.008** (0.003)	-	-0.005** (0.003)	-0.008** (0.003)
Adjusted R squared	0.798	0.797	0.795	0.809	0.808	0.804
Serial correlation test (LM)	0.070	0.090	0.180	0.380	0.450	0.840

Each equation is a panel regression with 334 observations. (-1) shows the lag of the variable. Figures in parentheses are standard errors. Standard errors are corrected for heteroscedastic errors by using the White (1980) heteroscedasticity-robust method. The Lagrange Multiplier (LM) tests serial correlation for one lag.
* The coefficient is significant at the 10 percent level.
** The coefficient is significant at the 5 percent level.

TABLE 5.15: Estimation Results for the United Kingdom's Two-Digit Sectors

VARIABLE NAME	COEFFICIENT					
	Total investment			Investment in machinery&equipment		
	(1)	(2)	(3)	(1)	(2)	(3)
Real exchange rate	0.725** (0.4286)	0.8169** (0.4216)	0.8186** (0.4035)	0.8107** (0.4153)	0.6522 (0.3623)	-0.7782 (0.7089)
Real exchange rate volatility	-1.9754** (0.6631)	-2.3113** (0.6169)	-2.3104** (0.5937)	-1.8575** (0.6079)	-1.9586** (0.5392)	1.0808 (1.3552)
Real interest rate	-0.0089 (0.0372)	0.0063 (0.0362)	0.0066 (0.0091)	0.0331 (0.0347)	0.0046 (0.008)	-0.0233 (0.022)
Real interest rate volatility	-0.0136 (0.0338)	-0.0426** (0.0253)	-0.0427** (0.0228)	-0.0486** (0.0303)	-0.0392** (0.0194)	0.0876 (0.1211)
Inflation rate	-0.0108 (0.0263)	-0.0002 (0.0256)	-	0.0197 (0.0238)	-0.0309** (0.0104)	-
Inflation rate volatility	-0.0388** (0.0225)	-	-	-0.0014 (0.0237)	-	-
Openness of the economy (-1)	1.1204* (0.8329)	1.4941** (0.7844)	1.4968** (0.7838)	1.3448** (0.8222)	0.0628 (0.1445)	-0.0110 (0.2004)
Growth rate of real GDP (-1)	0.0359** (0.0183)	0.0432** (0.0175)	0.0433** (0.0116)	0.0507** (0.0176)	0.0448** (0.0188)	0.0424** (0.0205)
Growth rate of value added (-1)	0.0036** (0.0022)	0.0038** (0.0022)	0.0038** (0.0021)	0.0037** (0.0017)	-0.0011** (0.0006)	-0.001** (0.0006)
Investment in fixed assets (-1)	0.4708** (0.0804)	0.4656** (0.0836)	0.4656** (0.0842)	-	-	-
Investment in machinery and equipment (-1)	-	-	-	0.461** (0.088)	0.4685** (0.09009)	0.4732** (0.090)
Time trend	-21.324** (10.495)	-22.684** (10.458)	-22.747** (8.894)	-20.535** (10.075)	-	-23.39** (8.253)
Time trend squared	0.0053** (0.0026)	0.0057** (0.0026)	0.0057** (0.002)	0.0051** (0.0025)	-	-0.005** (0.002)
Adjusted R squared	0.891	0.890	0.891	0.910	0.794	0.794
Serial correlation test (LM)	2.996	2.971	2.925	1.625	1.580	1.360

Each equation is a panel regression with 126 observations for total and 188 observations for machinery and equipment investments. (-1) shows the lag of the variable. Figures in parentheses are standard errors. Standard errors are corrected for heteroscedastic errors by using the White (1980) heteroscedasticity-robust method. The Lagrange Multiplier (LM) tests serial correlation for one lag.
* The coefficient is significant at the 10 percent level.
** The coefficient is significant at the 5 percent level.

TABLE 5.16: Estimation Results for the United Kingdom's Three-Digit Sectors

VARIABLE NAME	COEFFICIENT					
	Total investment			Investment in machinery&equipment		
	(1)	(2)	(3)	(1)	(2)	(3)
Real exchange rate	0.6867* (0.4667)	0.8167** (0.4606)	0.6713** (0.3918)	0.9350** (0.4013)	0.9948** (0.3924)	0.7379** (0.3431)
Real exchange rate volatility	-1.4041* (0.7922)	-1.4458** (0.7366)	-1.5278** (0.7278)	-1.2153** (0.7045)	-1.4025** (0.6588)	-1.546* 0.6668)
Real interest rate	0.0155 (0.0397)	0.0341 (0.0385)	0.0079 (0.0088)	0.0439 (0.0342)	0.0525* (0.0324)	0.0061 (0.0077)
Real interest rate volatility	-0.0265 (0.0319)	-0.0620** (0.0255)	-0.0523** (0.0220)	-0.0486* (0.0296)	-0.0650** (0.0222)	-0.047** (0.0211)
Inflation rate	0.0051 (0.0258)	0.0179 (0.0249)	-	0.0258 (0.0226)	-0.0318* (0.0215)	-
Inflation rate volatility	-0.0462** (0.0255)	-	-	-0.0213 (0.0239)	-	-
Openness of the economy (-1)	1.2729* (0.9597)	1.7409** (0.8844)	1.5303** (0.7819)	1.4889** (0.8476)	1.7061** (0.7718)	1.3311** (0.6887)
Growth rate of real GDP (-1)	0.0357** (0.0192)	0.0453** (0.0185)	0.0351** (0.0109)	0.016** (0.0165)	0.0560** (0.0155)	0.0379** (0.0093)
Growth rate of value added (-1)	0.0021* (0.0014)	0.0021* (0.0013)	0.0022* (0.0014)	0.0016** (0.0013)	0.0016 (0.0013)	0.0017 (0.0014)
Investment in fixed assets (-1)	0.5012** (0.0802)	0.5024** (0.0798)	0.5028** (0.0802)	-	-	-
Investment in machinery and equipment (-1)	-	-	-	0.4722** (0.0819)	0.4723** (0.0815)	0.4743** (0.0821)
Time trend	-24.737** (12.318)	-26.680** (12.2814)	-21.312** (9.088)	-24.603** (10.5157)	-25.494** (10.4378)-	-15.99** (8.3861)
Time trend squared	0.0062** (0.0031)	0.0067** (0.003)	0.0053** (0.0022)	0.0061** (0.0026)	0.0064** (0.0026)	0.004** (0.0021)
Adjusted R squared	0.836	0.835	0.835	0.863	0.863	0.863
Serial correlation test (LM)	5.64	5.173	4.952	0.900	0.872	0.591

Each equation is a panel regression with 392 observations for total and 188 observations for machinery and equipment investments. (-1) shows the lag of the variable. Figures in parentheses are standard errors. Standard errors are corrected for heteroscedastic errors by using the White (1980) heteroscedasticity-robust method. The Lagrange Multiplier (LM) tests serial correlation for one lag.
* The coefficient is significant at the 10 percent level.
** The coefficient is significant at the 5 percent level.

TABLE 5.17: Estimation Results for the United States' Two-Digit Sectors

VARIABLE NAME	COEFFICIENT					
	Total investment			Investment in machinery&equipment		
	(1)	(2)	(3)	(1)	(2)	(3)
Real exchange rate	0.6430** (0.1226)	0.6786** (0.0967)	0.4743** (0.0939)	0.6579** (0.1231)	0.6796** (0.0971)	0.4225** (0.0954)
Real exchange rate volatility	-0.3235 (0.5134)	-0.4185 (0.4805)	-0.0709 (0.4895)	-0.2463 (0.5215)	-0.3049 (0.4829)	0.0891 (0.5053)
Real interest rate	-0.0323** (0.0076)	-0.0352** (0.0064)	-0.0193** (0.0054)	-0.0331** (0.0082)	-0.0348** (0.0067)	-0.0156 (0.0058)
Real interest rate volatility	0.0543* (0.0346)	0.0629** (0.0339)	-0.0130** (0.0232)	0.0655** (0.0336)	0.0708** (0.0314)	-0.0212 (0.0223)
Inflation rate (-1)	-0.0286** (0.0131)	-0.0346** (0.0089)	-	-0.0369** (0.0139)	-0.0406 (0.8787)	-
Inflation rate volatility	-0.0154 (0.0267)	-	-	-0.0094 (0.0282)	-	-
Openness of the economy (-1)	7.6999** (2.1585)	8.1545** (1.8330)	4.8909** (1.6990)	8.9324** (2.2252)	9.2114** (1.8962)	5.3542** (1.7514)
Growth rate of real GDP (-1)	-	-	-	-	-	-
Growth rate of value added (-1)	0.0032** (0.0015)	0.0034** (0.0015)	0.0025** (0.0014)	0.0029 (0.0015)	0.003** (0.0015)	0.0021** (0.0014)
Investment in fixed assets (-1)	0.4666** (0.0948)	0.0034** (0.0015)	0.3276** (0.0937)	-	-	-
Investment in machinery and equipment (-1)	-	-	-	0.4480** (0.0972)	0.4476** (0.0975)	0.3041** (0.1002)
Time trend	-	-	-	-	-	-
Time trend squared	-	-	-	-	-	-
Adjusted R squared	0.931	0.932	0.925	0.936	0.936	0.928
Serial correlation test (LM)	0.0019	0.0101	3.773	0.321	0.280	2.812

Each equation is a panel regression with 117 observations. (-1) shows the lag of the variable. Figures in parentheses are standard errors. Standard errors are corrected for heteroscedastic errors by using the White (1980) heteroscedasticity-robust method. The Lagrange Multiplier (LM) tests serial correlation for one lag.
 * The coefficient is significant at the 10 percent level.
 ** The coefficient is significant at the 5 percent level.

TABLE 5.18: Estimation Results for the United States' Three-Digit Sectors

VARIABLE NAME	COEFFICIENT					
	Total investment			Investment in machinery&equipment		
	(1)	(2)	(3)	(1)	(2)	(3)
Real exchange rate	0.6275** (0.1170)	0.7093** (0.9708)	0.3497** (0.0908)	0.7034** (0.1166)	0.7576** (0.0993)	0.3872** (0.0860)
Real exchange rate volatility	-0.6644* (0.4160)	-0.8696** (0.3980)	-0.5278* (0.4104)	-0.2711 (0.4366)	-0.4076 (0.4117)	0.0799 (0.4240)
Real interest rate	-0.0326** (0.0068)	-0.0391** (0.0055)	-0.0139** (0.0038)	-0.0346** (0.0071)	-0.0390** (0.0058)	-0.0135** (0.0039)
Real interest rate volatility	0.1000** (0.0355)	0.1190** (0.0359)	0.0058 (0.0270)	0.0788** (0.0334)	0.0915** (0.0329)	-0.0212 (0.0252)
Inflation rate (-1)	-0.0376** (0.0118)	-0.0508** (0.0083)	-	-0.0417** (0.0121)	-0.0505** (0.0083)	-
Inflation rate volatility	-0.0339* (0.0248)	-	-	-0.0225 (0.0259)	-	-
Openness of the economy (-1)	7.4531** (1.9529)	8.4735** (1.7137)	2.9550** (1.6186)	9.4030** (2.0017)	10.081** (1.7873)	4.5320** (1.6334)
Growth rate of real GDP (-1)	-	-	-	-	-	-
Growth rate of value added (-1)	0.0020** (0.0009)	0.0022** (0.0008)	0.0016** (0.0009)	0.0015* (0.0009)	0.0016** (0.0009)	0.0011** (0.0010)
Investment in fixed assets (-1)	0.6658** (0.0676)	0.6639** (0.0677)	0.5939** (0.0687)	-	-	-
Investment in machinery and equipment (-1)	-	-	-	0.6163** (0.0732)	0.6149** (0.0734)	0.5490** (0.0752)
Time trend	-	-	-	-	-	-
Time trend squared	-	-	-	-	-	-
Adjusted R squared	0.929	0.929	0.923	0.933	0.933	0.928
Serial correlation test (LM)	1.371	1.285	0.123	1.460	1.376	0.0590

Each equation is a panel regression with 364 observations. (-1) shows the lag of the variable. Figures in parentheses are standard errors. Standard errors are corrected for heteroscedastic errors by using the White (1980) heteroscedasticity-robust method. The Lagrange Multiplier (LM) tests serial correlation for one lag.
* The coefficient is significant at the 10 percent level.
** The coefficient is significant at the 5 percent level.

VI

Empirical Results and Implications
Including "Openness" of Each Sector

6.1 Introduction

This chapter presents the second set of estimation results introducing variables measuring the "openness" of each sector into the regressions. This provides an opportunity to analyze the export and import exposure of the individual sectors in conjunction with real investment in the manufacturing sectors. As mentioned in Section 3.4, regressions that do not include the export and import share of the sectors may underestimate the effects of real exchange rates and real exchange rate volatility on investment expenditures.

Interaction variables defined by these export and import shares of the sectors are multiplied by the real exchange rates and real exchange rate volatility and are included in equations (1) through (3). These estimates may be even stronger than those obtained in Chapter 5. The estimation procedure is the same as in Chapter 5. The dependent variables are total investment and investment in machinery and equipment. Estimations were obtained for two- and three-digit ISIC manufacturing sectors.

6.2 Estimation Results Including Sector-Specific Foreign Trade Data

In this section, estimation results of the regressions including sector-specific foreign trade data are presented for Finland, Germany, the United Kingdom, and the United States.

6.2.1 Estimation Results for Finland

The estimation results for two- and three-digit manufacturing sectors of Finland are reported in Tables 6.1 and 6.2 respectively. The estimation period covers the periods 1982 to 1991, for two-digit sectors, and 1985 to 1991, for three-digit sectors.

The estimation results support the hypothesis that real exchange rate volatility has depressing effects on investment spending. The regressions using three-digit level sector data show this negative effect better than the regressions using two-digit level sector data. The coefficient of the variable that measures foreign trade exposure of the sector has a negative sign and is statistically significant in the regressions using three-digit level data.

The export and import exposure of the sector do not have statistically significant effects on investment spending. The export and import exposure coefficients are statistically insignificant in the regressions.

Real interest rate volatility coefficients are positively significant in the regressions using two-digit level data and in equations (1) and (2) using three-digit level total investment data. This result shows that real interest rate volatility stimulates investment, which is contrary to theory. Inflation rate volatility coefficient is positively significant in the regression using three-digit level total investment data. They are statistically insignificant in the other regressions.

The real interest rate coefficients are negatively significant in the regressions using three-digit level sector data. The inflation rate coefficients are negatively significant in the regressions as expected.

The growth rate of the real GDP is dropped from the regressions due to collinearity with the growth rate of value added. The growth rate of value added coefficients are negatively significant in the regressions, which was unexpected. The coefficients of the lagged dependent variables are statistically significant in all regressions as expected.

The LM test indicated no residual serial correlation. The White (1980) test indicated heteroscedastic errors. Hence, all standard errors are corrected for heteroscedasticity.

6.2.2 Estimation Results for Germany

The estimation results for the German two-digit manufacturing sectors are reported in Table 6.3.[1] The estimation period covers the period 1982 to 1991.

The estimation results support the hypothesis that real exchange rate volatility has negatively significant effects on real investment. The coefficient of the variable that measures foreign trade exposure of the sector is negatively significant in the regressions using total investment data.

The coefficient of the variable that measures export exposure of the sector is negatively significant only in equation (3) using total investment data. This result supports the hypothesis that real exchange rate appreciations depress investment in net exporting sectors. The coefficient of the variable that measures import exposure of the sector is positively significant only in equation (2) using total investment data. This result implies that real exchange rate appreciations stimulate investment in the sectors that depend heavily on imported inputs. But, in general, changes in the real exchange rate levels have no statistically significant effects on sectoral investment.

Other volatility measures, that is, real interest rate volatility and inflation rate volatility, have no depressing effects on investment spending. The real interest rate coefficients are negatively significant in the regressions using total investment data and in equation (3) using investment in machinery and equipment data. The inflation rate coefficients are negatively significant in all regressions as expected.

The growth rate of the real GDP is dropped from the regression due to collinearity with the growth rate of value added. The growth rate of value added coefficients are positively significant in all regressions as expected. The coefficients of the lagged dependent variables are positively significant in all regressions as expected.

The LM test indicated no residual serial correlation. The White (1980) test indicated heteroscedastic errors. Hence, all standard errors are corrected for heteroscedasticity.

6.2.3 Estimation Results for the United Kingdom

The estimation results for the United Kingdom's two- and three-digit manufacturing sectors are reported in Tables 6.4 and 6.5 respectively. The estimation period covers the period 1979 to 1988.

The estimation results support the hypothesis that real exchange rate volatility has depressing effects on sectoral investment. The coefficient of the variable that measures foreign trade exposure of the sectors has a negative sign and is statistically significant in all regressions. Real exchange rate volatility depresses investment when the foreign trade share of the sectors increases.

The coefficient of the variable that measures export exposure of the sector is negatively significant only in equation (3) using investment in machinery and equipment data at the three-digit level. This result indicates that an appreciation of the real exchange rate depresses investment in net exporting sectors. The coefficient of the variable that measures import exposure of the sector is positively significant in all regressions as expected. This result indicates that an appreciation of real exchange rate increases investment when import share of the sectors increases. This result is also consistent with results found in Chapter 5. In Chapter 5, the coefficient of the real exchange was found to be positively significant in all regressions. This shows that the United Kingdom's manufacturing sectors are mostly import-oriented.

Real interest rate volatility coefficients are negatively significant in the regressions without inflation rate and inflation rate volatility. Inflation rate volatility coefficients are negatively significant in all regressions as expected.

Other coefficients have the expected signs. The real interest rate coefficients are negatively significant in all regressions as expected. The inflation rate coefficients are negatively significant in all regressions as expected.

The growth rate of the real GDP is dropped from the regressions due to collinearity with the growth rate of value added. The growth rate of value added coefficients are positively significant as expected. When the profitability, which is proxied by the growth rate of value added, of the sectors increases, investment expenditures increase. The coefficients of the lagged dependent variables are positively significant in all regressions as expected.

The LM test indicated no residual serial correlation except for the regressions using the three-digit level total investment data. The White (1980) test indicated heteroscedastic errors. Hence, all standard errors are corrected for heteroscedasticity.

6.2.4 Estimation Results for the United States

The estimation results for the United States' two- and three-digit manufacturing sectors are reported in Tables 6.6 and 6.7 respectively. The estimation period covers the period 1980 to 1992.

The estimation results do support the hypothesis that real exchange rate volatility has depressing effects on sectoral investment. Although regressions using two-digit sector level data mask the effects of the real exchange rates and real exchange rate volatility on investment, regressions using three-digit level sector data present robust results. Real exchange rate volatility coefficients are negatively significant as expected in the theory. This result shows that real exchange rate volatility has depressing effects on investment when the foreign trade share of the sectors increases.

The coefficient of the variable that measures export exposure of the sector is negatively significant in the regressions as expected in the theory. Real exchange rate appreciations depress investment in net exporting sectors through reducing both foreign and domestic demand for domestic goods. The coefficient of the variable that measures import exposure of the sectors is positively significant in all regressions as expected in the theory. Real exchange rate appreciations increase investment in the sectors that use heavily imported inputs.

Real interest rate volatility coefficients are positively significant in all regressions, which is contrary to the expected values. Inflation rate volatility coefficients are negatively significant only in the regressions using three-digit level sector data. Since two-year inflation rate volatility causes collinearity, one-year inflation rate volatility is used in the estimation.

The real interest rate coefficients are negatively significant in all regressions as expected. The inflation rate coefficients are statistically insignificant in all regressions.

The growth rate of the real GDP is dropped from the regressions due to collinearity with the growth rate of value added. The growth rate of value added and the lag of the dependent variables coefficients are positively significant in all regressions.

The LM test indicated collinearity, when two-year inflation rate volatility was included in the regressions. Using one-year inflation rate volatility in the regressions solved this problem. The White (1980) test indicated heteroscedastic errors. Hence, all standard errors are corrected for heteroscedasticity.

6.3 Conclusion

In this chapter, the effects of real exchange rates and real exchange rate volatility on sectoral investment are examined using the variables measuring the "openness" of each sector in the regressions. As explained in Section 3.4, the regressions, which do not include the export and import exposure of the sectors, may underestimate the effects of real exchange rate changes and real exchange rate volatility on investment spending.

The estimation results presented in this chapter support this hypothesis. The estimation results including interactive variables show robust effects of real exchange rates and real exchange rate volatility on sectoral investment of the examined countries. The foreign trade exposure has depressing effects on sectoral investment in all countries. Real exchange rate volatility affects investment spending negatively when foreign trade share of the sectors increases.

The export exposure of the sectors has negatively significant effects on investment. Real exchange rate appreciations decrease investment when export share of the sectors increases. In the same way, the import exposure of the sectors has positively significant effects on investment. Real exchange rate appreciation stimulates investment when the import share of the sectors increases.

Contrary to Campa and Goldberg (1995) and Goldberg (1993), this study shows that real exchange rate volatility has depressing effects on investment in the U.S manufacturing sectors using interaction variables in the regressions. The estimation results also show that the United States and the United Kingdom manufacturing sectors are mostly import-oriented. Hence, real exchange rate appreciations expand investment in the manufacturing sectors of the United States and the United Kingdom.

NOTES

1. Investment data for the three-digit manufacturing sectors is not available. For that reason, only investment in the two-digit manufacturing sectors is used in the estimation.

TABLE 6.1: Estimation Results for Finland 's Two-Digit Sectors Including Export and

Import Share of Sectors

VARIABLE NAME	COEFFICIENT					
	Total investment			Investment in machinery&equipment		
	(1)	(2)	(3)	(1)	(2)	(3)
Export share of production * real exchange rate	-8.0792 (12.7586)	-8.6719 (11.3594)	11.9257* (9.2331)	-14.7597 (11.8033)	-13.1438 (10.8658)	-2.0202 (7.8606)
Import share of production * real exchange rate	-1.5315 (2.8244)	-1.6621 (2.4984)	2.8386* (2.0306)	-3.1333 (2.6071)	-2.7772 (2.3949)	-0.3580 (1.7607)
Foreign trade share of production * real exchange rate volatility	7.8098 (12.7801)	8.4013 (11.4031)	-12.1572* (9.2820)	14.7786 (11.8547)	13.1651 (10.9058)	1.8267 (7.9695)
Real interest rate	0.0367 (0.1266)	0.0323 (0.1056)	-0.0076 (0.1028)	-0.0130 (0.1207)	-0.0012 (0.0943)	0.0466 (0.0936)
Real interest rate volatility	0.1055** (0.0259)	0.1059** (0.0261)	0.0986** (0.0261)	0.1053** (0.0247)	0.1042** (0.0249)	0.0299** (0.0077)
Inflation rate	-9.4454** (2.8434)	-9.390** (2.6211)	-	-5.5014** (2.7503)	-5.6505** (2.6041)	-
Inflation rate volatility	-0.0021 (0.0339)	-	-	0.0060 (0.030)	-	-
Growth rate of value added (-1)	-0.0051** (0.0026)	-0.0051** (0.0026)	-0.0054** (0.0029)	-0.0015 (0.0027)	-0.0015 (0.0027)	-0.0014 (0.0032)
Investment in fixed assets (-1)	0.1917** (0.0927)	0.1909** (0.0922)	0.2125** (0.1079)	-	-	-
Investment in machinery and equipment (-1)	-	-	-	0.2965** (0.1071)	0.2992** (0.1066)	0.2993** (0.1213)
Time trend	-88.00** (29.907)	-87.180** (24.544)	-34.368** (19.904)	-57.402** (29.092)	-59.676** (25.132)	-
Time trend squared	0.0221** (0.007)	0.0219** (0.006)	0.0086** (0.005)	0.0014** (0.007)	0.0150** (0.006)	-
Adjusted R squared	0.721	0.725	0.698	0.766	0.769	0.702
Serial correlation test (LM))	3.144	3.114	1.516	2.187	1.983	1.524

Each equation is a panel regression with 90 observations. (-1) shows the lag of the variable. Figures in parantheses are standard errors. Standard errors are corrected for heteroscedastic errors by using the White (1980) heteroscedasticity-robust method. The Lagrange Multiplier (LM) tests serial correlation for one lag.
* The coefficient is significant at the 10 percent level.
** The coefficient is significant at the 5 percent level.

TABLE 6.2: Estimation Results for Finland's Three-Digit Sectors Including Export and

Import Share of Sectors

VARIABLE NAME	COEFFICIENT					
	Total investment			Investment in machinery & equipment		
	(1)	(2)	(3)	(1)	(2)	(3)
Export share of production* real exchange rate	-0.0713 (0.1567)	-0.0634 (0.1566)	-0.0883 (0.1631)	-0.0332 (0.074)	-0.0318 (0.0734)	-0.3807 (0.0754)
Import share of production* real exchange rate	0.0268 (0.0625)	0.0494 (0.0593)	0.0346 (0.0583)	-0.0229 (0.0251)	-0.0187 (0.0234)	-0.0235 (0.0240)
Foreign trade share of production * real exchange rate volatility	-7.022** (3.4493)	-9.929** (3.1774)	-7.5319** (3.107)	-4.8567** (2.5866)	-5.4075** (2.1647)	-4.684** (2.092)
Real interest rate (-1)	-0.428** (0.1214)	-0.305** (0.0913)	-0.0267** (0.0292)	-0.1312 (0.1070)	-0.1077* (0.0793)	-0.025** (0.0192)
Real interest rate volatility	0.6236** (0.2668)	0.3117* (0.1896)	-0.233 (0.1435)	0.0376 (0.2538)	-0.0221 (0.1805)	-
Inflation rate	-0.362** (0.1126)	-0.255** (0.0874)	-	-0.0961 (0.0974)	-0.0755 (0.0732)	-
Inflation rate volatility	0.2356* (0.1518)	-	-	-0.0449 (0.1303)	-	-
Growth rate of value added (-1)	-0.0065** (0.003)	-0.007** (0.0033)	-0.0071** (0.0034)	-0.0041** (0.0024)	-0.0043** (0.0024)	-0.004** (0.0024)
Investment in fixed assets (-1)	0.2475** (0.106)	0.283** (0.118)	0.2838** (0.1186)	-	-	-
Investment in machinery and equipment (-1)	-	-	-	0.3457** (0.0775)	0.3442** (0.0781)	0.3372** (0.080)
Time trend	-0.1541** (0.039)	-0.143** (0.039)	26.014** (4.676)	-0.042** (0.020)	-0.0409** (0.019)	-0.022** (0.013)
Time trend squared	0.00007** (0.0002)	0.0007** (0.0001)	-0.0065** (0.0011)	-0.042** (0.0209)	0.00002** (0.000009)	0.00001** (0.000006)
Adjusted R squared	0.532	0.531	0.521	0.699	0.702	0.702
Serial correlation test (LM)	6.633	6.335	0.982	3.397	1.370	1.524

Each equation is a panel regression with 140 observations. (-1) shows the lag of the variable. Figures in parentheses are standard errors. Standard errors are corrected for heteroscedastic errors by using the White (1980) heteroscedasticity-robust method. The Lagrange Multiplier (LM) tests serial correlation for one lag.
* The coefficient is significant at the 10 percent level.
** The coefficient is significant at the 5 percent level.

TABLE 6.3: Estimation Results for Germany's Two-Digit Sectors Including Export and Import Share of Sectors

VARIABLE NAME	COEFFICIENT					
	Total investment			Investment in machinery&equipment		
	(1)	(2)	(3)	(1)	(2)	(3)
Export share of production * real exchange rate	-0.0395 (0.0920)	-0.0672 (0.0840)	-0.1825** (0.0837)	0.0171 (0.1148)	0.0292 (0.1057)	-0.0998 (0.0891)
Import share of production * real exchange rate	0.0402 (0.0361)	0.0482* (0.0361)	0.0223 (0.0363)	0.0089 (0.060)	0.0060 (0.0602)	-0.0091 (0.0504)
Foreign trade share of production * real exchange rate volatility	-3.1001** (1.0342)	-2.8875** (1.7756)	-1.2184* (0.8523)	-1.2865 (1.1798)	-1.3771 (1.1695)	-0.2398 (0.9256)
Real interest rate (-1)	-0.0293** (0.2983)	-0.0354** (0.0134)	-0.0364** (0.0121)	-0.0135 (0.0197)	-0.0108 (0.0179)	-0.0260** (0.0127)
Real interest rate volatility	-0.0499 (0.0616)	-0.0649 (0.0568)	-0.0359 (0.055)	-0.0425 (0.0769)	-0.0360 (0.0705)	-
Inflation rate	-0.0371** (0.0074)	-0.039** (0.0073)	-	-0.0225** (0.0102)	-0.021** (0.010)	-
Inflation rate volatility	0.0370 (0.0369)	-	-	-0.0154 (0.0406)	-	-
Growth rate of value added (-1)	0.0121** (0.0026)	0.0120** (0.0026)	0.0078** (0.0027)	0.0087** (0.0031)	0.0088** (0.0032)	0.0045** (0.0030)
Investment in fixed assets (-1)	0.6428** (0.0775)	0.6310** (0.0763)	0.4157** (0.0932)	-	-	-
Investment in machinery and equipment (-1)	-	-	-	0.6226** (0.1017)	0.6247** (0.1027)	0.3929** (0.1243
Time trend	-	-	26.014** (4.6768)	-	-	17.140** (6.4585)
Time trend squared	-	-	-0.0065** (0.0011)	-	-	-0.0043** (0.0016)
Adjusted R squared	0.888	0.888	0.901	0.863	0.865	0.883
Serial correlation test (LM)	3.313	3.20	0.982	3.397	3.125	0.837

Each equation is a panel regression with 77 observations. (-1) shows the lag of the variable. Figures in parentheses are standard errors. Standard errors are corrected for heteroscedastic errors by using the White (1980) heteroscedasticity-robust method. The Lagrange Multiplier (LM) tests serial correlation for one lag.
* The coefficient is significant at the 10 percent level.
** The coefficient is significant at the 5 percent level.

TABLE 6.4: Estimation Results for the United Kingdom's Two-Digit Sectors Including

Export and Import Share of Sectors

VARIABLE NAME	COEFFICIENT					
	Total investment			Investment in machinery&equipment		
	(1)	(2)	(3)	(1)	(2)	(3)
Export share of production * real exchange rate	0.1007 (0.1188)	0.1825 (0.1054)	0.1556** (0.1015)	0.0795 (0.0839)	0.1360** (0.0757)	0.0666 (0.0773)
Import share of production * real exchange rate	0.0830** (0.0147)	0.0834** (0.0145)	0.0763** (0.0139)	0.0771** (0.0129)	0.0759** (0.0127)	0.0715** (0.0171)
Foreign trade share of production * real exchange rate volatility	-0.8666** (1.3537)	-2.244** (1.1079)	-1.6331* (1.0826)	-0.5674 (0.8916)	-1.4495** (0.7811)	-1.1574** (0.8682)
Real interest rate	-0.0 641 (0.0236)	-0.0618** (0.0255)	-0.0095* (0.0066)	-0.0565** (0.0203)	-0.0520** (0.0213)	-0.0141** (0.0057)
Real interest rate volatility	0.0202 (0.0382)	-0.0285 (0.0315)	-0.074** (0.0139)	0.0044 (0.0295)	-0.0312 (0.0252)	-0.0586** (0.0157)
Inflation rate	-0.0490** (0.0215)	-0.044** (0.0221)	-	-0.0474** (0.0171)	-0.042** (0.0174)	-
Inflation rate volatility	-0.0789** (0.0247)	-	-	-0.0524** (0.0194)	-	-
Growth rate of value added (-1)	0.0021 (0.0016)	0.003** (0.0017)	0.0040** (0.0017)	0.0031** (0.0014)	0.0038** (0.0014)	0.005** (0.0017)
Investment in fixed assets (-1)	0.4046** (0.0905)	0.4291** (0.1037)	0.4812** (0.1033)	-	-	-
Investment in machinery and equipment	-	-	-	0.3926** (0.1017)	0.4351** (0.1032)	0.5823** (0.0928)
Time trend	-24.985** (9.001)	-24.084** (9.671)	-37.034** (7.8125)	-22.48** (8.30)	-22.34** (8.5122)	-
Time trend squared	0.0062** (0.0022)	0.006** (0.0024)	0.0093** (0.0019)	0.0056** (0.0020)	0.0056** (0.0021)	-
Adjusted R squared	0.901	0.890	0.886	0.923	0.919	0.897
Serial correlation test (LM)	0.786	0.317	0.201	1.627	0.895	0.148

Each equation is a panel regression with 90 observations. (-1) shows the lag of the variable. Figures in parentheses are standard errors. Standard errors are corrected for heteroscedastic errors by using the White (1980) heteroscedasticity-robust method. The Lagrange Multiplier (LM) tests serial correlation for one lag.
  * The coefficient is significant at the 10 percent level.
 ** The coefficient is significant at the 5 percent level.

TABLE 6.5: Estimation Results for the United Kingdom's Three-Digit Sectors Including

Export and Import Share of Sectors

VARIABLE NAME	COEFFICIENT					
	Total investment			Investment in machinery&equipment		
	(1)	(2)	(3)	(1)	(2)	(3)
Export share of production *real exchange rate	-0.0585 (0.1222)	-0.0365 (0.1197)	-0.0606 (0.1143)	-0.1240 (0.1187)	-0.1012 (0.1155)	-0.1980** (0.1139)
Import share of production * real exchange rate	0.1664** (0.070)	0.1782** (0.0697)	0.1763** (0.0699)	0.1719** (0.0665)	0.1822** (0.0669)	0.2092** (0.0684)
Foreign trade share of production * real exchange rate volatility	-2.0499** (1.1401)	-2.6845** (1.023)	-1.5112** (0.9705)	-1.4983** (1.0341)	-2.099** (0.9216)	-1.2982** (0.8721)
Real interest rate	-0.0576** (0.0193)	-0.0658** (0.0191)	-0.0125* (0.0095)	-0.0625** (0.0159)	-0.0698** (0.0156)	-0.0190** (0.0073)
Real interest rate volatility	0.0234 (0.0293)	0.0017 (0.0238)	-0.058** (0.0215)	0.02632 (0.0270)	0.0053 (0.0213)	-0.0504** (0.0144)
Inflation rate	-0.0322** (0.0155)	-0.039** (0.0155)	-	-0.0391** (0.0129)	-0.046** (0.0127)	-
Inflation rate volatility	-0.0380** (0.0228)	-	-	-0.0359* (0.0222)	-	-
Growth rate of value added (-1)	0.0016 (0.0014)	0.0016 (0.0014)	0.0019** (0.0014)	0.001 (0.0014)	0.0010** (0.0014)	0.0015** (0.0015)
Investment in fixed assets (-1)	0.4148** (0.1116)	0.4271** (0.1076)	0.4667** (0.1124)	-	-	-
Investment in machinery and equipment (-1)	-	-	-	0.3063** (0.1034)	0.3238** (0.0980)	0.4076** (0.0908)
Time trend	-	-	-	-	-	-
Time trend squared	-	-	-	-	-	-
Adjusted R squared	0.818	0.817	0.814	0.849	0.849	0.841
Serial correlation test (LM)	1.438	0.997	0.537	0.998	0.411	0.0624

Each equation is a panel regression with 280 observations. (-1) shows the lag of the variable. Figures in parentheses are standard errors. Standard errors are corrected for heteroscedastic errors by using the White (1980) heteroscedasticity-robust method. The Lagrange Multiplier (LM) tests serial correlation for one lag.
  * The coefficient is significant at the 10 percent level.
  ** The coefficient is significant at the 5 percent level.

TABLE 6.6:   Estimation Results for the United States' Two-Digit Sectors Including

Export and Import Share of Sectors

VARIABLE NAME	COEFFICIENT					
	Total investment			Investment in machinery&equipment		
	(1)	(2)	(3)	(1)	(2)	(3)
Export share of production * real exchange rate	-0.0273 (0.1236)	-0.0283 (0.1259)	-0.0272 (0.1256)	0.0594 (0.1319)	0.0597 (0.1327)	0.0597 (0.133)
Import share of production * real exchange rate	0.0057** (0.0019)	0.0061** (0.0018)	0.0060** (0.0017)	0.0066** (0.0019)	0.0068** (0.0018)	0.0068** (0.0017)
Foreign trade share of production * real exchange rate volatility	-2.2585 (1.9157)	-2.8857* (1.7756)	-3.0644** (1.5678)	-1.9366 (2.0985)	-2.2834 (1.8873)	-2.2866* (1.6774)
Real interest rate	-0.0104** (0.0054)	-0.0103** (0.0054)	-0.0112* (0.004)	-0.0093** (0.0054)	-0.0093** (0.0054)	-0.0093** (0.0042)
Real interest rate volatility	0.0537* (0.0359)	0.0562* (0.0358)	-0.063** (0.0139)	0.0643** (0.0338)	0.0657** (0.0334)	-
Inflation rate (-1)	0.0042 (0.0091)	0.0023 (0.0091)	-	0.0011 (0.0088)	-	-
Inflation rate volatility	-0.0277 (0.0302)	-	-	-0.0151 (0.0326)	-	-
Growth rate of value added (-1)	0.0039** (0.0016)	0.004** (0.0016)	0.0041** (0.0015)	0.0035** (0.0017)	0.0036** (0.0017)	0.0036** (0.0016)
Investment in fixed assets (-1)	0.4707** (0.1035)	0.4621** (0.1028)	0.4762** (0.0887)	-	-	-
Investment in machinery and equipment (-1)	-	-	-	0.4233** (0.1056)	0.4199** (0.1052)	0.4202** (0.0963)
Time trend	-	-	-	-	-	-
Time trend squared	-	-	-	-	-	-
Adjusted R squared	0.931	0.913	0.914	0.918	0.919	0.930
Serial correlation test (LM)	0.284	0.693	0.0223	0.177	0.0078	0.0074

Each equation is a panel regression with 117 observations. (-1) shows the lag of the variable. Figures in parentheses are standard errors. Standard errors are corrected for heteroscedastic errors by using the White (1980) heteroscedasticity-robust method. The Lagrange Multiplier (LM) tests serial correlation for one lag.
 *   The coefficient is significant at the 10 percent level.
 ** The coefficient is significant at the 5 percent level.

TABLE 6.7: Estimation Results for the United States' Three-Digit Sectors Including

Export and Import Share of Sectors

VARIABLE NAME	COEFFICIENT					
	Total investment			Investment in machinery&equipment		
	(1)	(2)	(3)	(1)	(2)	(3)
Export share of production *real exchange rate	-0.1437** (0.0837)	-0.1485** (0.0897)	-0.1529** (0.0903)	-0.1304* (0.0832)	-0.1331* (0.0871)	-0.1357* (0.0873)
Import share of production * real exchange rate	0.0464** (0.0273)	0.0572** (0.0284)	0.0576** (0.0291)	0.0376** (0.0225)	0.0449** (0.0234)	0.0455** (0.0240)
Foreign trade share of production * real exchange rate volatility	-1.9284** (0.8142)	-2.7730* (0.8935)	-2.5014** (0.8194)	-1.6565** (0.6747)	-2.2214** (1.7355)	-2.0175** (0.6750)
Real interest rate	-0.0130** (0.0044)	-0.012** (0.0044)	-0.0084** (0.003)	-0.0115** (0.0045)	-0.0108** (0.0045)	-0.0081** (0.0032)
Real interest rate volatility	0.0940** (0.0324)	0.0959** (0.0326)	0.0632** (0.0135)	0.0808** (0.0304)	0.0822** (0.0305)	0.0571** (0.0127
Inflation rate (-1)	-0.0048 (0.0069)	-0.0086 (0.0072)	-	-0.0039 (0.0068)	-0.0065 (0.007)	-
Inflation rate volatility	-0.0716** (0.0257)	-	-	-0.0478** (0.0258)	-	-
Growth rate of value added (-1)	0.0018** (0.0009)	0.002** (0.0091)	0.0019** (0.0009)	0.0013** (0.001)	0.0014** (0.001)	0.0013** (0.001)
Investment in fixed assets (-1)	0.6601** (0.0638)	0.6469** (0.0635)	0.6306** (0.0596)	-	-	-
Investment in machinery and equipment (-1)	-	-	-	0.5998** (0.0715)	0.5903** (0.0718)	0.5794** (0.0691)
Time trend	-	-	-	-	-	-
Time trend squared	-	-	-	-	-	-
Adjusted R squared	0.922	0.920	0.920	0.925	0.924	0.924
Serial correlation test (LM)	3.704	0.304	0.0945	2.195	0.315	0.145

Each equation is a panel regression with 364 observations. (-1) shows the lag of the variable. Figures in parentheses are standard errors. Standard errors are corrected for heteroscedastic errors by using the White (1980) heteroscedasticity-robust method. The Lagrange Multiplier (LM) tests serial correlation for one lag.
* The coefficient is significant at the 10 percent level.
** The coefficient is significant at the 5 percent level.

VII

Summary and Conclusions

After the collapse of the Bretton Woods fixed exchange rate system, negative implications of exchange rate volatility led European countries to adopt a target zone system in March 1979. This new exchange rate system was called the Exchange Rate Mechanism (ERM) of the European Monetary System (EMS).

One of the main reasons for the establishment of the ERM of the EMS was to create a stable exchange rate environment and by do so, to induce investment and trade in Europe. Artis and Taylor (1994) and Grauwe and Verfaille (1988) showed that the ERM was successful in reducing the volatility of intra-EMS exchange rates. Grauwe and Verfaille also showed that the ERM helped to increase trade among the EMS versus non-EMS countries. Since no empirical study has been done regarding the effects of real exchange rate volatility on European investment, it is impossible to make any decision about the effects of real exchange rate volatility on investment in Europe.

This study analyzed the effects of real exchange rate volatility on investment in manufacturing sectors for countries under quasi-fixed (that is, the EMS) and flexible exchange rate systems by answering the question, "In which system does real exchange rate volatility have negatively significant effects on sectoral investment?"

While exchange rates fluctuates within narrow margins in the ERM of the EMS, they fluctuate randomly in the flexible exchange rate system. Therefore, real exchange rate volatility should not have depressing effects on investment in the EMS, while it should have depressing effects on investment in the flexible exchange rate system.

The existing empirical studies do not support the hypothesis that real exchange rate volatility has depressing effects on real investment. For instance, Goldberg (1993) examined the effects of real exchange rate volatility on investment in U.S. industry.

The results do not support the hypothesis that real exchange rate volatility has depressing effects on investment in U.S. industry. Since the United States is large and has a relatively closed economy, the response of investment decisions to exchange rate levels and volatility may not be very high. Pindyck and Solimano (1993) examined the effects of real exchange rate volatility, as well as inflation rate and inflation rate volatility using aggregate investment data pooled across countries. They concluded that the inflation rate has depressing effects on investment but that real exchange rate volatility does not. They used pooled aggregate investment data, which may mask different patterns at the sectoral level.

Therefore, the objective of this study was to test the effects of the levels and volatility of real exchange rates on investment at the sectoral level for open economies. Because volatility can be transferred from exchange rates to interest rates, the effects of real interest rate volatility, in addition to real exchange rate volatility, are examined if there is a volatility transfer. The United States is also included for comparison to previous studies. Sectoral investment data used in this study is obtained from the OECD. To the best of my knowledge, this study is unique in using this data source for empirical study of sectoral investment behavior.

For the four countries of Finland, Germany, the United Kingdom, and the United States, foreign trade data, as well as investment data are available at the sectoral level. Sector-specific foreign trade data provide the opportunity to analyze effects of export and import exposure on investment, while controlling for export and import exposure in each sector.

In the theoretical part of the study, using option pricing techniques, it is proved that real exchange rate volatility causes break-even real exchange rate to get higher for export-oriented sectors and lower import-oriented sectors. Thus the zone of "inaction" increases, and real investment falls as volatility increases regardless of whether the sector is an export-oriented or import-oriented sector.

In the empirical part of the study, the investment equations are estimated using investment in fixed assets, as well as investment in machinery and equipment for two- and three-digit ISIC manufacturing sectors. The OECD investment data does not provide enough observations to estimate either a cross-sectional or time-series equation. Therefore, annual time-series data are pooled across sectors for each country separately. The estimation period covers the period 1979 to 1993. The starting point is the inception of the ERM of the EMS. The estimation technique is the Ordinary Least Squares (OLS), and sector-specific fixed effects are included by adding sector dummies into the regressions. The regressions are estimated with and without including sector-specific foreign trade variables.

The estimation results support the hypothesis that real exchange rate volatility has depressing effects on sectoral investment of the countries in the flexible exchange rate system, while it has no depressing effects on sectoral investment of the countries in the EMS. Countries. The only EMS country in which real exchange rate volatility has depressing effect on sectoral investment is Germany. Since the ERM of the EMS imposes low volatility in exchange rates, it is not easy to measure uncertainty through exchange rates in the EMS countries, except Germany.

Although Germany is a member of the ERM of the EMS, the German mark is freely floating against the non-EMS currencies, and German trade with non-EMS countries is extensive. Therefore, real exchange rate volatility may have depressing effects on real investment in this case. Artis and Taylor (1994) also found that while the EMS was successful in reducing the exchange rate volatility between the EMS countries, the volatility of the German mark against the non-EMS currencies has not changed during that period. In the EMS countries, inflation rate volatility has depressing effects on sectoral investment in France and Italy; and the inflation rate has depressing effects on investment in Belgium, Germany, and the Netherlands.

The estimation results do not show any conclusive empirical evidence concerning volatility transfer from exchange rates to interest rates in the EMS countries. Real interest rate volatility has robust depressing effects on real investment only in the French manufacturing sectors, which supports the hypothesis developed by Ingersoll and Ross (1992).

Real exchange rate volatility has depressing effects on sectoral investment of the countries in the flexible exchange rate system, that is, Finland, Norway, the United Kingdom, and the United States. The estimation results, including export- and import-orientation and "openness" to international trade of each sector, capture the effects of the real exchange rates and real exchange rate volatility on sectoral investment precisely. These estimation results show that the United States and the United Kingdom manufacturing sectors are mostly import-oriented. Therefore, the real exchange rate appreciations cause sectoral investment expansions in the U.S. and United Kingdom manufacturing sectors. This result is consistent with Goldberg (1993) and Campa and Goldberg (1995).

Contrary to Goldberg (1993) and Campa and Goldberg (1995), the empirical results of this study show negatively significant effects of real exchange rate volatility on investment in the U.S. manufacturing sectors.

Pindyck and Solimano (1993) noted that the effects of volatility variables, that is, real exchange rate volatility, inflation rate volatility, and real interest rate volatility, on investment spending are analyzed accurately by using sectoral level data. The empirical results of this study also support their predictions. Disaggregated data provides conclusive evidence about the effects of volatility variables on investment spending.

Appendix

A.1 Value of the Plant Under Real Exchange Rate Uncertainty

In this part, value of the plant under real exchange rate uncertainty is determined for import-oriented firms. First, equation (3.45) is evaluated. In order to express dV, Ito's Lemma is used.

$$dV = V_e \, de + \frac{1}{2} V_{ee} \, de^2 \qquad (A.1)$$

where $V_e = dV / de$ and $V_{ee} = d^2 V / de^2$. Substituting equations (3.2) and (3.3) into (A.1) gives

$$dV = V_e \, (\sigma e dz) + \frac{1}{2} V_{ee} \, (\sigma^2 e^2 \, dt) \qquad (A.2)$$

Taking expectations of both sides of equation (A.2) yields

$$E \, (dV) = \frac{1}{2} V_{ee} \, \sigma^2 \, e^2 \, dt \qquad (A.3)$$

Hence, equation (3.45) can be written as

$$rV dt = \frac{1}{2} V_{ee} \, \sigma^2 \, e^2 \, dt + \lambda \, (\bar{e} - e) dt \qquad (A.4)$$

Simplifying and rearranging equation (A.4) yields the following ordinary differential equation

$$\frac{\sigma^2}{2} e^2 V_{ee} - rV + \lambda \bar{e} - \lambda e = 0 \qquad (A.5)$$

The proposed solution to this ordinary differential equation is as follows

$$A_1 e^{\alpha_1} + A_2 e + A_3 = V \qquad (A.6)$$

Taking the second derivative of equation (A.6) with respect to e and putting it into equation (A.5) yields $A_2 = -\lambda / r$, and $A_3 = \lambda \bar{e} / r$. Then the value of the plant, $V(e)$, is

$$V(e) = A_1 e^{\alpha_1} + \lambda \frac{(\bar{e} - e)}{r} \qquad e < \bar{e} \qquad (A.7)$$

The roots are either $\alpha_1 < 0$ or $\alpha_1 > 1$. Boundary condition (3.50) indicates that if the real exchange rate is extremely small, then the value of the plant, V, is like a perpetuity discounted by interest rate r, and the value of the option to shut down, $A_1 e^{\alpha_1}$, approaches zero. Therefore, it must be true that $\alpha_1 > 1$. Next, equation (3.46) is evaluated.

$$rVdt = E(dV) \qquad e > \bar{e} \qquad (A.8)$$

$$rVdt = \frac{\sigma^2}{2} V_{ee} e^2 dt \qquad e > \bar{e} \qquad (A.9)$$

Rearranging equation (A.9) gives

$$\frac{\sigma^2}{2} e^2 V_{ee} - rV = 0 \qquad e > \bar{e} \qquad (A.10)$$

Again, V must satisfy this ordinary differential equation. The proposed solution is

$$A_4 e^{\alpha_2} = V \qquad (A.11)$$

Taking the second derivative of equation (A.11) with respect to e and substituting into equation (A.10) gives

$$\left[\frac{\sigma^2}{2} \alpha_2 (\alpha_2 - 1) - r \right] A_4 e^{\alpha_2} = 0 \qquad (A.12)$$

Since $\lim e \to 0$, $V(e) = 0$, then $\beta_2 < 0$. Now the coefficients A_1 and A_4 are found by using boundary conditions (3.48) and (3.49). These boundary conditions yield the following equalities

$$A_1 \bar{e}^{-\alpha_1} + \lambda \frac{(\bar{e} - \bar{e})}{r} = A_4 \bar{e}^{\alpha_2} \qquad (A.13)$$

$$\alpha_1 A_1 \bar{e}^{(\alpha_1 - 1)} + \frac{\lambda}{r} = \alpha_2 A_4 \bar{e}^{(\alpha_2 - 1)} \qquad (A.14)$$

Then, the value of the project can be written as follows

$$V(e) = \frac{\lambda}{r} \frac{\bar{e}^{-(1-\alpha_1)}}{(\alpha_1 - \alpha_2)} e^{\alpha_1} + \frac{\lambda}{r} (\bar{e} - e) \qquad e < \bar{e}$$

$$\qquad (A.15)$$

$$V(e) = \frac{\lambda}{r} \frac{\bar{e}^{-(1-\alpha_2)}}{(\alpha_1 - \alpha_2)} e^{\alpha_2} \qquad e > \bar{e}$$

A.2 The Value of Option to Invest in the Plant and Optimal Stopping Point

Assume a firm is waiting for new information about the real exchange rate. While waiting to build, there are no cash flows. Therefore, expected capital gains on the opportunity to invest are equal to the risk-free return on an investment of equivalent value, that is

$$rFdt = E(dF) \qquad (A.16)$$

By using Ito's Lemma, dF is expressed as

$$dF = F_e de + \frac{1}{2} F_{ee} de^2 \qquad (A.17)$$

Substituting equation (3.2) for de and equation (3.3) for de^2 yields

$$dF = F_e(\sigma edz) + \frac{1}{2} F_{ee}(\sigma^2 e^2 dt) \qquad (A.18)$$

Taking the expectations of equation (A.18) yield the following equation

$$E(dF) = \frac{1}{2} \sigma^2 e^2 F_{ee} dt \qquad (A.19)$$

Replacing $E(dF)$ in equation (A.16) with equation (A.19) gives

$$rF - \frac{1}{2} \sigma^2 e^2 F_{ee} = 0 \qquad (A.20)$$

Equation (A.20) is an ordinary differential equation, which is solved subject to boundary conditions (3.52), (3.53), and (3.54). The solution to equation (A.20) is given by

$$F(e^*) = b e^{\alpha_3} \qquad e > e^* \qquad \text{(A.21)}$$

Taking the second derivative of equation (A.21) with respect to e and substituting into equation (A.20) yields the following equation

$$\left[\frac{\sigma^2}{2} \alpha_3(\alpha_3 - 1) - r \right] b \, e^{\alpha_3} = 0 \qquad \text{(A.22)}$$

Boundary condition $V(e) = 0$ implies that $\alpha_3 < 0$. Hence, $\alpha_3 = \alpha_2$. Now the value of e^* and coefficient b are determined using the boundary conditions (3.53) and (3.54). At e^* these two conditions must meet

$$\frac{\lambda}{r} \frac{\bar{e}^{(1-\alpha_1)}}{(\alpha_1 - \alpha_2)} e^{\alpha_1} + \frac{\lambda}{r} (\bar{e} - e^*) - I = b \, e^{*\alpha_2} \qquad \text{(A.23)}$$

$$\alpha_1 \left[\frac{\lambda}{r} \frac{\bar{e}^{(1-\alpha_1)}}{(\alpha_1 - \alpha_2)} e^{*(\alpha_1 - 1)} \right] \left(-\frac{\lambda}{r} \right) + \frac{\lambda}{r} = \alpha_2 b e^{*(\alpha_2 - 1)} \qquad \text{(A.24)}$$

The coefficient b is determined from equation (A.24).

$$b = \frac{\lambda}{r} \left[\frac{\alpha_1}{\alpha_2} \frac{\bar{e}^{(1-\alpha_1)}}{(\alpha_1 - \alpha_2)} e^{*(\alpha_1 - \alpha_2)} - \frac{e^{*(1-\alpha_2)}}{\alpha_2} \right] \qquad \text{(A.25)}$$

Substituting (A.25) into (A.23) gives the following implicit equation that e^* must satisfy. This equation is as follows

$$\frac{\lambda}{r} \frac{\bar{e}^{(1-\alpha_1)}}{(\alpha_1 - \alpha_2)} \left(1 - \frac{\alpha_1}{\alpha_2} \right) e^{*\alpha_1} + \frac{\lambda}{r} \left(\frac{1}{\alpha_2} - 1 \right) e^* + \frac{\lambda}{r} \bar{e} - I = 0 \qquad \text{(A.26)}$$

Finally, the relationship between the volatility and the optimal stopping point, e^*, is determined. What does the effect of volatility increase have on e^*? Defining equation (A.26) as Ψ, I will prove that

$$\frac{de^*}{d\sigma^2} = -\frac{\Psi_{\sigma^2}}{\Psi_{e^*}} < 0 \qquad (A.27)$$

where Ψ_{σ^2} is the derivative of implicit function with respect to σ^2 and Ψ_{e^*} is the derivative of implicit function with respect to e^*. Ψ_{σ^2} and Ψ_{e^*} are derived to decide if $-\Psi_{\sigma^2}/\Psi_{e^*} < 0$. Ψ_{e^*} is derived as

$$\Psi_{e^*} = \frac{\lambda}{r}\left[-\frac{\alpha_1}{\alpha_2}\left(\frac{\bar{e}}{e^*}\right)^{(1-\alpha_1)} + \frac{1}{\alpha_2} - 1\right] > 0 \qquad (A.28)$$

when $\bar{e} = e^*$, this expression reaches its maximum. Using the definitions, $\alpha_1 = 1/2 + 1/2 (1 +8r / \sigma^2$ and $\alpha_2 = 1/2 - 1/2 (1 +8r/ \sigma^2)$, this implies that $\Psi_{e^*} = 0$. Ψ_{σ^2} is defined by chain differentiation

$$\Psi_{\sigma^2} = \Psi_{\alpha_1}\frac{d\alpha_1}{d\sigma^2} + \Psi_{\alpha_2}\frac{d\alpha_2}{d\sigma^2} \qquad where \quad \frac{d\alpha_2}{d\sigma^2} = -\frac{d\alpha_2}{d\sigma^2} \qquad (A.29)$$

Taking the derivatives of equation (A.26) with respect to α_1 and α_2 yields the following equations

$$\Psi_{\alpha_2} = e^*\frac{\lambda}{r}\left(\frac{1}{\alpha_2}\right)^2\left[\left(\frac{\bar{e}}{e^*}\right)^{(1-\alpha_1)} - 1\right] \qquad (A.30)$$

$$\Psi_{\alpha_1} = \left(-\frac{\lambda}{r\alpha_2}\right)\left[-\ln\bar{e} + \ln e^*\right]e^{*\alpha_1}\,\bar{e}^{(1-\alpha_1)} \qquad (A.31)$$

It was demonstrated earlier that $\alpha_1 > 1$ and $\alpha_2 < 0$. Using these facts and inspection of (A.30) and (A.31) show that $\Psi\alpha_1 > 0$ and and $\Psi\alpha_2 < 0$. Hence,

$$\left[-\Psi_{\alpha_1} + \Psi_{\alpha_2}\right] \frac{d\alpha_1}{d\sigma^2} = \Psi_{\sigma^2} \tag{A.32}$$

It is proven that $\Psi_e^* > 0$ and $\Psi_{\sigma^2} > 0$. Therefore, the following equality hold.

$$\frac{de^*}{d\sigma^2} = -\frac{\Psi_{\sigma^2}}{\Psi_{e^*}} < 0 \tag{A.33}$$

Bibliography

Abel, Andrew B. "Optimal Investment Under Uncertainty. " *American Economic Review*, March 1983, 73(1), pp. 228-233.

Abel, Andrew B. "Investment," in Benjamin M. Friedman, ed., *Handbook of Monetary Economics*, Volume II, The Netherlands: Elsevier Science Publishers B.V., 1991, pp. 753-778.

Abel, Andrew B., and Eberly, Janice C. "A Unified Model of Investment Under Uncertainty." *American Economic Review*, December 1994, 84(5), pp.1369-1384.

Aizenman, Joshua. "Exchange Rate Flexibility, Volatility, and Domestic and Foreign Direct Investment." *IMF Staff Papers*, December 1992, Vol. 39, No. 4, pp. 890-922.

Artis, Michael J., and Taylor, Mark P. "The Stabilizing Effect of the ERM on Exchange Rates and Interest Rates." *IMF Staff Papers*, March 1994, 41(1), pp. 123-148.

Baldwin, Richard. "Hysteresis in Import Prices: The Benchead Effect." *American Economic Review*, September 1988, 78(4), pp. 773-785.

Baldwin, Richard, and Krugman, Paul. "Persistent Trade Effects of Large Exchange Rate Shocks." *Quarterly Journal of Economics*, November 1989, 104(4), pp. 635-654.

Batiz, Francisco L. Rivera., and Batiz, Luis A. Rivera. *International Finance and Open Economy Macroeconomics*. New York: MacMillan Publishing Company, 1994.

Branson, William H., Litwack, James M. *Macroeconomics*. New York: Harper & Row Publishers, 1986.

Caballero, Ricardo J. "On the Sign of the Investment-Uncertainty Relationship." *American Economic Review*, March 1991, 81(1), pp. 279-288.

Caballero, Ricardo J., and Corbo, Vittorio. "The Effect of Real Exchange Rate Uncertainty on Exports: Empirical Evidence." *The World Bank Eonomic Review*, 1989, 3(2), pp. 263-278.

Caballero, Ricardo J., and Pindyck, Robert S. *Uncertainty, Investment, and Industry Evolution*. Massachusetts Institute of Technology Working Paper, 1995.

Campa, Jose, and Goldberg, Linda S. "Investment in Manufacturing, Exchange Rates and External Exposure." *Journal of International Economics*, May 1995, 38(3/4), pp. 297-320.

Clark, Peter, Bartolini, Leonardo, Bayoumi, Tamim, and Symansky, Steven. *Exchange Rates and Economic Fundamentals*. IMF Occasional Paper, December 1994, No.115, Washington DC.

Craine, Roger. "Risky Business: The Allocation of Capital." *Journal of Monetary of Economics*, March 1989, 23(1), pp. 201-218.

Deravi, M. Keivan, and Metghalchi, Massaud. "The European Monetary System: A Note." *Journal of Banking and Finance*, September 1988, 12(3), pp. 505-512.

Dixit, Avinash. (a) "Hysteresis, Import Penetration, and Exchange Rate Pass-through." *Quarterly Journal of Economics*, May 1989, 104(2), pp. 205-228.

Dixit, Avinash. (b) "Entry and Exit Decisions under Uncertainty." *Journal of Political Economy*, June 1989, 97(3), pp. 620-638.

Dixit, Avinash. "Investment and Hysteresis." *Journal of Economic Perspectives,* Winter 1992, 6(1), pp. 107-132.

Dornbush, Rudiger. "Exchange Rates and Prices." *American Economic Review*, March 1987, 77(1), pp. 93-106.

Duesenbery, J. S. *Income, Savings and the Theory of Consumer Behavior.* Cambridge, MA, 1958.

Edison, Hali J., and Fisher, Eric O'N. "A Long Run View of the European Monetary System." *Journal of International Money and Finance*, March 1991, 10, pp. 53-70.

Engel, Charles and Hakkio, Craig S. "Exchange Rate Regimes and Volatility." *Economic Review (Federal Reserve Bank of Kansas City)*, Third Quarter (1993), pp. 43-58.

Federal Reserve Bank of Chicago. *Readings in International Finance.* Chicago, Illinois, 1986.

Ferderer, J. Peter. "The Impact of Uncertainty on Aggregate Investment Spending: An Empirical Analysis." *Journal of Money Credit and Banking*, February 1993, Vol. 25, No. 1, pp. 30-47.

Fischer, Stanley. "Growth, Macroeconomics, and Development." *NBER, Macroeconomics Annual*, Cambridge, MA: The MIT Press, 1991, pp. 329-364.

Fischer, Stanley, and Modigliani, Franco. "Towards an Understanding of the Real Effects and Costs of Inflation." *Weltwirtschaftliches Archiv*, 1978, 114(4), pp. 810-832.

Frankel, Jeffrey and Meese, Richard. "Are the Exchange Rates Too Variable?" *NBER Macroeconomics Annual*, Cambridge, MA: The MIT Press, 1987, pp. 117-162.

Froot, Kenneth. "Multinational Corporations, Exchange Rates, and Direct Investment," in William H. Branson, ed., *International Policy Coordination and Exchange Rate Fluctuations*, NBER Project Report, Chicago: The University of Chicago Press, 1990.

Froot, Kenneth A., and Stein, Jeremy C. "Exchange Rates and Foreign Direct Investment: An Imperfect Capital Market Approach." *Quarterly Journal of Economics*, November 1991, 106(4), pp. 1191-1217.

Goldberg, Linda S. "Exchange Rates and Investment in the United States Industry." *The Review of Economics and Statistics*, November 1993, Vol. LXXV (4), pp. 575-588.

Goldberg, Linda S., and Kolstad, C. *Foreign Direct Investment, Exchange Rate Variability, and Demand Uncertainty.* Faculty Working Paper no. 93-158, Bureau of Economic and Business Research, University of Illinois at Urbana-Champaign (August 23, 1993).

Grauwe, Paul De, and Verfaille, Guy. "Exchange Rate Variability, and the European Monetary System, in R. Marston,ed., *Misalignment of Exchange Rates*, NBER Project Report, Chicago: The University of Chicago Press, 1988.

Greene, W. H. *Econometric Analysis.* New York: MacMillan, 1993.

Hall, Robert, and Jorgenson, Dale W. " Application of the Theory of Optimal Capital Accumulation," in Gary Fromm, ed., *Tax Incentives and Capital Spending*, Washington DC: Brookings Institution, 1971.

Hayashi, Fumio. "Tobin's Marginal q and Average q: A Neoclassical Interpretation." *Econometrica*, January 1982, 50(1), pp. 213-224.

Hildebrandt, Paula. "The Path to European Monetary Union." Economic Review (Federal Reserve Bank of Kansas City), March/April 1991, pp. 35-48.

Hsiao, Cheng. *Analysis of Panel Data.* Cambridge, England: Cambridge University Press, 1986.

Hubbard, R. Glenn. "Investment Under Uncertainty: Keeping One's Options Open." *Journal of Economic Literature*, December 1994, Vol. XXXII, pp. 816-1831.

IMF. *Exchange Rate Volatility and World Trade*. IMF Occasional Paper, No: 28, July, 1984.

Ingersoll, Jonathan, and Ross, Stephen. "Waiting to Invest: Investment Under Uncertainty." *Journal of Business*, January 1992, 65(1), pp. 1-29.

Jorgenson, Dale W. "Capital Theory and Investment Behavior." *American Economic Review*, May 1963 (Papers and Proceedings), 53(2), pp. 247-59.

Jorgenson, Dale W. "The Theory of Investment Behavior," in Robert Ferber, ed., *Determinants of Investment Behavior*, Cambridge, MA: NBER, 1967.

Keynes, John Maynard. *The General Theory of Employment, Interest and Money*. San Diego: Harcourt Brace Jovanovich, 1936.

Krugman, Paul. *Exchange Rate Instability*. Cambridge, MA: The MIT Press 1989.

Leahy, John V., and Whited, Toni M. "The Effects of Uncertainty on Investment: Some Stylized Facts." *Journal of Money Credit, and Banking*, February 1996, 28(1), pp. 64-83.

Levine, Ross, and Renelt David. "A Sensitivity Analysis of Cross-Country Growth Regressions." *American Economic Review*, September, 1992, 82(4), pp. 942-963

Luehrman, Timothy A. "Exchange Rate Changes and the Distribution of Industry Value." *Journal of International Business Studies*, 1991, 21, pp. 619-649.

Maddala, G. S. *Introduction to Econometrics*. New York: Macmillan Publishing Company, 1992.

Mankiw, N. Gregory. *Macroeconomics.* New York: Worth Publishers, 1994.

McDonald, Robert, and Siegel, Daniel. "The Value of Waiting to Invest." *Quarterly Journal of Economics,* November 1986, 101, pp. 707-728.

Odeh, H. S. *The Impact of Inflation on the Level of Economic Activity.* The Netherlands: Rotterdam University Press, 1968.

Pindyck, Robert S. "Irreversible Investment, Capacity Choice, and the Value of the Firm." *American Economic Review,* December 1988, 78(5), pp. 969-985.

Pindyck, Robert S. "Irreversibility, Uncertainty, and Investment." *Journal of Economic Literature,* September 1991, Vol. XXIX, pp. 1110-1148.

Pindyck, Robert S., and Solimano, Andres. "Economic Instability and Aggregate Investment." *NBER, Macroeconomics Annual,* Cambridge, MA: The MIT Press, 1993, pp. 259-303.

Pindyck, Robert S., and Dixit, Avinash. *Investment Under Uncertainty,* Princeton: Princeton University Press, 1994.

Richardson, David J. "Exchange Rates and U.S. Auto Competitiveness," in R. Marston, ed., *Misalignment of Exchange Rates,* NBER Project Report, Chicago: University of Chicago Press, 1988.

Serven, Luis, and Solimano, Andres. "Private Investment and Macroeconomic Adjustment: A Survey." *The World Bank Research Observer,* January 1992, 7(1), pp. 95-114.

Solimano, Andres. "How Private Investment Reacts to Changing Macroeconomic Conditions: The Case of Chile." PRE Working Paper 212, *World Bank, Country Economics Department,* Washington D.C, 1989.

Tobin, James. "A General Equilibrium Approach to Monetary Theory." *Journal of Money Credit and Banking*, February 1969, 1(1), pp. 15-29.

White, Halbert. "A Heteroscedasticity-Consistent Covariance Matrix Estimator and a Direct Test for Heteroscedasticity." *Econometrica*, May 1980, 48(4), pp. 817-838.

Wilson, George W. *Inflation*, Bloomington: Indiana University Press, 1982.

Index

Abel, Andrew, 15-16
Absorbing barrier, 48
Accelerator theory, 10, 11-12, 62
Aizenman, Joshua, 4, 24
Argentina, 21, 58
Artis, Michael J., 3, 38, 88, 135
Asymmetric cost, 16
Asymmetry, 32
Australia, 35
Average q, 14, 19
Baldwin, Richard, 25
Batiz, Francisco L. Rivera.
    and Luis A. Rivera , 24
Belgium, 6, 36, 84-85
Bolivia, 21, 58
Brazil, 21, 58, 62
Break-even rate,
    of exchange rate, 44, 45, 54,
    134
    of interest rate, 17
Bretton Woods, 35, 133
Brownian motion, 20, 43
Caballero, Ricardo J., 16, 20
Call option, 20, 41
Campa, Jose, 5, 25, 27-28, 37, 105,
    106, 123, 136
Canada, 33, 34, 35
Capital Asset Pricing Model
    (CAPM), 18
Capital gains, expected, 13, 44, 45,
    54

Cash flows, expected, 44, 45,
    48, 54, 55
Chile, 21, 58
CIF, 75, 77
Citibase, 67
Clark et al., 73
Competitiveness, price, 23, 29,
    36, 42, 73
COMPUSTAT, 18
Consumer Price Index (CPI), 75
Craine, Roger, 15, 16
Cross-sectional time-series
    data, 21, 22, 58, 67,
    70-71, 135
Denmark, 6, 36, 69, 82, 86
Differential equation, 46, 47
Dixit, Avinash, 20, 25, 42, 43
Duesenberry, J. S., 11
Durbin Watson statistic, 83
Economic instability indicators, 21
Engel, Charles, 24, 36
European Currency Unit
    (ECU), 3, 35
European Monetary System
    (EMS), 3-4, 35, 36, 67, 82,
    83-84, 107, 133, 135
EUROSTAT, 67
Exchange Rate Mechanism
    (ERM), 3, 35, 36, 133, 135

153